LUXURY HOTELS

SPA & WELLNESS

edited by Patrice Farameh & Martin Nicholas Kunz

teNeues

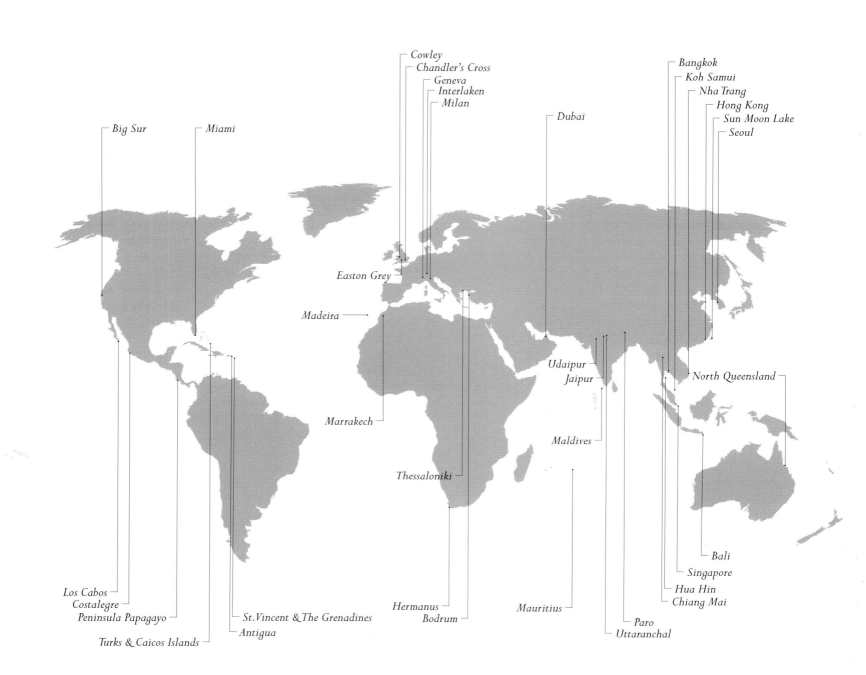

Cowley
Chandler's Cross
Geneva
Interlaken
Milan

Bangkok
Koh Samui
Nha Trang
Hong Kong
Sun Moon Lake
Seoul

Big Sur

Miami

Dubai

Easton Grey

Madeira

Marrakech

Udaipur
Jaipur

North Queensland

Maldives

Thessaloniki

Bali

Singapore

Los Cabos
Costalegre
Peninsula Papagayo

St.Vincent & The Grenadines

Hua Hin
Chiang Mai

Turks & Caicos Islands

Antigua

Hermanus
Bodrum

Mauritius

Paro
Uttaranchal

Luxury Hotels

SPA & WELLNESS

Rejuvenation Retreats

A world-class resort isn't complete without the presence of a signature spa specially designed to cultivate the body, mind and spirit. Guests who flock to these five-star retreats are no longer just buying hotel suites amidst luxurious surroundings for the sole pursuit of pampering. Today destination spas are for those who demand that the resort's main attraction is a comprehensive program relating to their physical and mental well-being.

These luxury resorts embrace advanced holistic treatments that concentrate on in-depth overall wellness. Integrated spas are not just about indulging the guest, but engaging all of the senses. From the moment a guest enters one of these architecturally elegant resorts, the restorative properties of its lavish surroundings sink in and uplift spirits before one even enters a treatment room. All of these spa retreats offer soul-soothing atmospheres within spectacular settings so well orchestrated, that each guest feels that it is part of a staged piece of the spa. Whether the breathtaking views are of turquoise waters, lush mountains and forests, or of sparkling cityscapes, it all comes together naturally to create an indulgent spa experience in harmony with the natural world. Even on the 11th floor of the Grand Hyatt in the heart of Hong Kong, the Plateau Spa equipped its rooftop garden with fountains, pools, and a waterfall to provide the ultimate Zen-like calm.

The spas featured in this book are totally deluxe and truly service oriented. Many offer treatments in isolated spa suites or on private terraces with tranquil views of nature. Each resort adheres to a strict philosophy of white-glove service with warm hospitality where personalized attention is the norm, such as 24-hour butlers who make sure that a guest doesn't have to lift more than a finger, even when it comes to wiping their own sunglasses by the pool. In the Amanjena Resort in Morocco, where the employee outnumbers the guest five to one, each staff member is trained to greet every guest personally with their name, and remembers their personal preferences as well. For those in the quest for self-improvement, all of these spas offer personalized service with therapists who are trained to sense what a person needs, or is looking for.

In all of these resorts, it is mandatory that the guest leaves the PDA at home, and lets the full-service concierge be the day planner. Nothing is too much trouble. A hopeless romantic at The Western Cape can have a massage for two arranged on a private balcony overlooking the surrounding natural beauties of a Nature Reserve. A guest at the One&Only Le Touessrok can have Thalasso treatments outdoors while immersed within the incense of aromatic flowers from the surrounding exotic gardens and trees, or on the beach at The Como Shambhala spa in the Maldives listening to the soothing rhythmic sound of retreating waves.

These health and beauty hideaways offer more than just a holiday, a bronzed glow from the Mediterranean sun, or a lower golf handicap. This is an escape to a deeply relaxing environment to recapture a youthful glow and ageless vitality at the edge of paradise. Many of the spas featured serve the whole person by incorporating self-awareness with physical fitness. From the lady of leisure staying at El Tamarindo who wants a healing herbal mud wrap in the oxygenated cool air of the nearby rainforests, to the athlete who wants to physically recover with meditative movements in the birthplace of Yoga in the Ananda Spa in the Himalayan mountains, the diversity of these spa programs are expansive to meet a wide variety of needs. Each guest will walk away with a well body and mind from the therapeutic properties offered by each of the featured world-class spa resorts. The general philosophy shared by each spa is that inward is where to look for true peace.

It's hard to say what makes a spa truly exceptional, but whatever that elusive element is, these luxury spas featured in this book have it. These recuperative retreats are luxuriously illustrated on each page, including a descriptive short text that introduces these state-of-the-art destinations where each guest goes deeper to places of renewal.

Patrice Farameh

Jungbrunnen

Ein Weltklasseresort ist unvollständig wenn es kein herausragendes Spa besitzt, das eigens dafür geschaffen wurde, Körper, Seele und Geist zu pflegen. Gäste, die in diese Fünf-Sterne-Refugien strömen, wollen nicht länger allein für eine Hotelsuite in luxuriöser Umgebung zahlen, um sich nur verwöhnen zu lassen. Heute sind Spas Reiseziele für diejenigen, die von der Hauptattraktion eines Hotels ein umfassendes Programm für ihr körperliches und seelisches Wohlergehen verlangen.

Diese Luxusresorts bieten ausgefeilte, ganzheitliche Behandlungen für vollständige Rundum-Wellness. Die zu den Hotels gehörenden Spas verwöhnen nicht nur den Gast, sondern sprechen alle seine Sinne an. Von dem Moment an, da ein Gast eines dieser architektonisch eleganten Urlaubsresorts betritt, wird diesem die erholsame Wirkung der verschwenderischen Umgebung bewusst und seine Stimmung hebt sich, bevor er auch nur einen Behandlungsraum betreten hat. Eine beruhigende Atmosphäre schaffen diese Spas durch spektakuläre Inszenierung, die so durchdacht sind, dass sich jeder als Teil eines Schauspiels fühlt. Ob es nun der atemberaubende Blick auf tür-kisfarbene Gewässer, großartige Berge und Wälder oder glänzende Stadtlandschaften ist — alles fügt sich harmonisch zusammen und bietet eine Spa-Erlebnis im Einklang mit der natürlichen Welt. Selbst in der elften Etage des Grand Hyatt im Herzen von Hongkong rüstete das Plateau Spa seinen Dachgarten mit Brunnen, Bassins und einem Wasserfall aus, um die ultimative Gelassenheit des Zen zu schaffen.

Die Spas, die in diesem Buch vorgestellt werden, sind wahre Luxusoasen und extrem serviceorientiert. Viele bieten Behandlungen in separaten Bäder-Suiten oder auf privaten Terrassen mit beruhigendem Blick auf die Natur an. Jedes Resort hält strikt an der Philosophie fest, perfekte Betreuung mit herzlicher Gastfreundschaft zu verbinden, um ein Höchstmaß an persönlichen Service zu bieten. So sorgen z.B. Butler rund um die Uhr dafür, dass ein Gast nicht mehr als nur den Finger heben muss, selbst wenn es nur darum geht, sich am Pool die Sonnenbrille putzen zu lassen. Im Amanjena Resort in Marokko, wo auf einen Gast fünf Angestellte kommen, sind die Angestellten angewiesen, jeden Gast mit seinem Namen zu begrüßen und sich dessen persönliche Vorlieben zu merken. Denjenigen, die an sich arbeiten wollen, bieten all diese Spas ein auf sie persönlich zugeschnittenes Training mit Therapeuten an, die darin ausgebildet sind zu erkennen, was jemand braucht oder sucht.

In all diesen Resorts ist es geradezu Pflicht, dass die Gäste ihren PDA zu Hause lassen und die Wohlfühl-Experten die Tagesplanung übernehmen. Nichts macht zu viel Mühe. Ein hoffnungsloser Romantiker kann im The Western Cape eine Massage für zwei auf einem privaten Balkon mit Blick auf die umgebenden Schönheiten eines Natur-schutzgebietes genießen. Ein Gast im One&Only Le Touessrok kann im Freien Thalasso-Behandlungen erhalten, während er sich den Düften der Blumen und Bäume aus den umgebenden exotischen Gärten hingibt, oder am Strand des The Como Shambala Spa auf den Malediven dem beruhigenden Rauschen des Meeres lauschen.

Diese Refugien der Schönheit und Gesundheit bieten mehr als nur einen Urlaub, mediterrane Sonnenbräune oder ein niedrigeres Golf-Handicap. Sie ermöglichen die Flucht in eine zutiefst entspannende Umgebung, um jugendliche Ausstrahlung und alterslose Vitalität am Rande des Paradieses wieder zu finden. Viele der Spas in diesem Buch kümmern sich um den Menschen als Ganzes, indem sie Selbsterkenntniss und Fitness vereinen. Ob für die Entspannung suchenden Dame, die sich ins El Tamarindo begibt und nach heilenden Schlammpackungen in der sauerstoffreichen, kühlen Luft des nahen Regenwaldes verlangt, oder den Sportler, der sich physisch mit Meditation am Geburtsort des Yoga im Ananda Spa im Himalaya erholen will, die Wellness-Angebote sind weit gefächert, um den unterschiedlichsten Ansprüchen gerecht zu werden. Jeder Gast wird sich bei seiner Abreise mit Leib und Seele wohl fühlen dank der therapeutischen Behandlungen, die von jedem der hier vorgestellten Häuser der Spitzen-klasse angeboten werden. Die übereinstimmende Philosophie in all diesen Spas besagt, dass man den wahren Frieden nur im Inneren finden kann.

Es ist schwierig zu sagen, was ein Wellness-Hotel wirklich außergewöhnlich macht, aber was auch immer dieses schwer definierbare Element sein mag — die in diesem Buch vorgestellten Luxusresorts haben es. Die erholsamen Refugien, aus denen jeder Gast wiedergeboren zurückkommt, werden durch viele Bilder und kurze, informa-tive Texte vorgestellt.

Patrice Farameh

Des lieux où se ressourcer

Un complexe hôtelier de grand standing ne saurait être complet aujourd'hui sans la présence d'un centre spa de renommée conçu pour la culture du corps et de l'esprit. Les hôtes qui affluent vers ces refuges cinq étoiles ne cherchent plus seulement des suites d'hôtel dans un environnement somptueux juste dans le but de se faire choyer. Aujourd'hui les spas sont destinés à tous ceux qui demandent que la principale attraction de leur lieu de villégiature soit un vaste programme axé sur leur bien-être physique et mental.

Ces complexes de luxe proposent des thérapies holistiques avancées qui se concentrent sur un bien-être profond et général. Les centres spas intégrés ne se contentent pas uniquement de choyer le client, mais d'éveiller tous ses sens. Dès qu'un hôte pénètre dans l'un de ces élégants temples de l'architecture, les propriétés réparatrices de l'environnement luxueux commencent à agir et mettent de bonne humeur même avant d'entrer dans une salle de traitement. Tous ces refuges offrent une atmosphère apaisante pour l'âme avec des paysages spectaculaires si bien choisis que chaque hôte a le sentiment que cela fait partie d'une mise en scène du centre spa. Que la vue époustouflante soit des eaux turquoises, des montagnes et forêts opulentes, des paysages urbains étincelants, tout contribue à créer une expérience thermale agréable et réparatrice en harmonie avec le monde naturel. Même au 11ème étage du Grand Hyatt au cœur de Hong Kong, le Plateau Spa est équipé d'un jardin sur le toit avec des fontaines, des piscines et une cascade pour offrir un calme zen absolu.

Les centres spas présentés dans cet ouvrage sont des établissement de grand luxe et véritablement orientés sur le service. Bon nombre d'entre eux offrent des traitements dans des suites thermales isolées ou sur des terrasses privées avec des vues tranquilles sur le paysage. Chaque complexe adhère à une philosophie stricte du service avec des gants blancs et une hospitalité chaleureuse où l'attention personnalisée est la norme, comme par exemple des majordomes 24 h sur 24 qui veillent à ce que le client n'ait pas à lever le petit doigt, ne serait-ce que pour essuyer ses lunettes de soleil au bord de la piscine. A l'Amanjena Resort au Maroc, où les employés sont cinq fois plus nombreux que les clients, chaque membre du personnel a été formé pour accueillir chaque invité personnellement par son nom et se rappeler ses préférences personnelles également. Pour ceux en quête d'un amélioration personnelle, toutes ces centres spas offrent des services personnalisés avec des thérapeutes formés pour déceler ce dont une personne a besoin ou ce qu'elle cherche.

Dans tous ces complexes, il est obligatoire de laisser chez soi son PDA et de confier au concierge le soin de planifier le programme de la journée. Tout est possible. Un romantique invétéré logé au The Western Cape peut demander un massage pour deux personnes sur un balcon privé avec vue sur le magnifique paysage d'une réserve naturelle. Un autre client séjournant au One&Only Le Touessrok peut souhaiter une thalassothérapie à l'air libre immergé dans le parfum intense des fleurs aromatiques des jardins et arbres exotiques environnants ou écouter sur la plage du The Como Shambhala spa aux Maldives le bruit rythmé et apaisant des vagues.

Ces refuges dédiés à la santé et à la beauté offrent plus que des vacances, un bronzage au soleil de la Méditerranée ou un meilleur handicap au golf. C'est une fuite vers un environnement de grande détente pour retrouver un éclat juvénile et une vitalité sans âge que l'on ne trouve qu'aux confins du paradis. De nombreux centres spas décrits se consacrent à toute la personne avec des activités destinées à mieux de se connaître et à améliorer son état physique. De la femme désœuvrée séjournant à l'El Tamarindo qui désire un bain de boue aux herbes guérisseuses dans l'air frais et vivifiant des forêts tropicales, à l'athlète qui veut retrouver sa forme physique par des mouvements méditatifs là où est né le yoga à l'Ananda Spa dans les montagnes de l'Himalaya, la diversité des programmes permet de répondre à des besoins très variés. Chaque client repartira en bonne santé physique et mentale grâce aux propriétés thérapeutiques offertes par ces complexes spas de grand standing ici décrits. La même philosophie générale est partagée par chacun de ces centres : ce n'est qu'à l'intérieur de soi que l'on trouve la paix véritable.

Il est difficile de définir ce qui rend exceptionnel un centre spa, mais quoi que ce soit, les spas ici présentés le possèdent assurément. Ces lieux de retraite réparateurs sont illustrés par des photos somptueuses à chaque page, y compris un bref descriptif de ces destinations où chaque hôte s'enfonce encore plus profondément dans un univers où il peut se ressourcer.

Patrice Farameh

Lugares para rejuvenecer

Un resort de primera clase no es tal si no cuenta con su spa característico especialmente diseñado para cultivar el cuerpo, la mente y el espíritu. Los huéspedes que acuden en gran número a estos refugios de cinco estrellas ya no buscan solamente suites en lugares lujosos donde ser mimados. Los spa de hoy en día son para quienes exigen que la principal atracción del resort sea un amplio programa relacionado con su bienestar físico y mental.

Estos resorts de lujo incluyen tratamientos holísticos de avanzada que se concentran en el bienestar profundo y general. Los spa integrados no buscan solamente mimar al huésped, sino despertar todos sus sentidos. Desde el momento en que el visitante entra a uno de estos resorts de elegancia arquitectónica, las propiedades reparadoras del esplendor del entorno comienzan a hacer efecto y le mejoran el ánimo, aun antes de que entre a una sala de tratamiento. Todos estos refugios ofrecen ambientes que alivian el alma, con paisajes espectaculares tan bien elegidos que cada visitante siente que es parte de una representación de una escena del spa. Ya sea que la vista imponente sea de aguas cristalinas, montañas o bosques exuberantes, o de paisajes urbanos deslumbrantes, todo se combina naturalmente para hacer posible una experiencia placentera y reparadora en armonía con la naturaleza. Incluso en el piso once del hotel Grand Hyatt, en el corazón de Hong Kong, el Plateau Spa equipó el jardín de la azotea con fuentes, piscinas y una catarata para asegurar la calma zen más absoluta.

Los spa presentados en este libro son absolutamente de lujo y están verdaderamente orientados hacia el servicio. Muchos ofrecen tratamientos en suites aisladas o terrazas privadas con vista a la naturaleza. Todos los resorts adhieren a una estricta filosofía de servicio con guante blanco y cálida hospitalidad, en la que la atención personalizada es la norma, como, por ejemplo, mediante mayordomos las 24 horas del día que se aseguran de que los huéspedes no muevan un dedo, aunque solo se trate de limpiar sus propias gafas de sol al borde de la piscina. En el Amanjena Resort de Marruecos, donde hay cinco empleados por huésped, todos los miembros del personal saludan a los huéspedes por el nombre y recuerdan sus preferencias personales. Para quienes están en busca de la superación personal, todos estos spa ofrecen servicios personalizados de terapeutas entrenados para descubrir qué necesita o busca cada persona.

En todos estos resorts es obligatorio dejar el PDA en casa y aceptar que el concierge multiservicio defina el programa del día. Todo es posible. En el The Western Cape, un romántico empedernido puede solicitar un masaje para dos en un balcón privado con vista a la belleza salvaje de una Reserva Natural. Un huésped del One&Only Le Touessrok puede recibir un tratamiento thalasso al aire libre, inmerso en el intenso aroma de las flores de los jardines y árboles exóticos circundantes, o en la playa, en el spa The Como Shambhala de las Maldivas, escuchando el sonido rítmico y tranquilizador de las olas.

Estos refugios de salud y belleza ofrecen mucho más que unas vacaciones, un bronceado del mediterráneo o un mejor handicap de golf. Se trata de una escapada a un lugar intensamente relajante para recobrar el brillo juvenil y la vitalidad sin edad que solo se encuentra en el límite del paraíso. Muchos de estos spa están orientados a la persona en su totalidad, incluyendo actividades para conocerse mejor a uno mismo y mejorar el estado físico. Desde la dama del ocio que se hospeda en El Tamarindo y quiere que la envuelvan con un lodo de hierbas reparadoras mientras disfruta del aire fresco y oxigenado de la selva tropical vecina, hasta el deportista que quiere recuperarse físicamente haciendo movimientos de meditación en la cuna del Yoga, en el Ananda Spa del Himalaya, la diversidad de estos programas abarca múltiples necesidades. Cada huésped vuelve a casa con su cuerpo y mente en buen estado gracias a las propiedades terapéuticas ofrecidas por cada uno de estos resorts de primera clase. La filosofía general de los spa es que es necesario mirar hacia adentro para encontrar la paz verdadera.

Es difícil decir qué es lo que hace que un spa sea verdaderamente excepcional, pero sea cual fuere ese elemento, los spa de lujo presentados en este libro seguramente lo tienen. Para cada uno de estos refugios reparadores se incluye una lujosa ilustración en cada página, junto con un breve texto descriptivo que presenta estos destinos de avanzada, en los que los huéspedes penetran en espacios de renovación.

Patrice Farameh

Centri ringiovanimento

Un luogo di villeggiatura di classe internazionale non è completo se non equipaggiato di un Spa firmato e creato specialmente per la cura del corpo, dello spirito e della mente. Gli ospiti che affluiscono a tali luoghi di ritiro da cinque stelle non solo comprano delle suites in alberghi immersi in ambienti di lusso per il solo piacere di viziarsi con raffinatezza. Oggi le mete dei luoghi di villeggiatura sono destinate a coloro che si aspettano come attrazione principale un programma completo e ricco di contenuti per curare il loro benessere fisico e mentale.

Questi luoghi lussuosi includono avanzati trattamenti complessivi che sono mirati accuratamente al benessere totale. Tali centri di benessere integrati non solo viziano l'ospite, ma si prendono cura di tutti i suoi sensi. Nel momento in cui l'ospite entra in uno di questi Spa con la loro eleganza architettonica, si accorge delle loro capacità riposanti e ricreative e la sua mente si rallegra ancora prima di entrare nei singoli centri di trattamento. Tutti questi luoghi di ritiro offrono un'atmosfera che addolcisce l'animo con messe in scena così ben organizzate da regalare ad ogni ospite l'impressione di far parte dello spettacolare luogo di benessere. Che sia un panorama mozzafiato di acque turchesi, grandiosi montagne e foreste o scintillanti vedute della città, il tutto si unisce naturalmente per creare una dolce esperienza nel centro di benessere, in armonia con la natura. Addirittura all'undicesimo piano del Grand Hyatt nel cuore di Hong Kong, il Plateau Spa con il suo giardino pensile sul tetto con fontane, piscine e una cascata regala l'ultimativa calma a modo Zen.

I Spa rappresentati in questo libro sono totalmente deluxe e realmente orientati al servizio. Molti offrono trattamenti in separate suites o su terrazze private con tranquilli panorami della natura. Ogni centro di benessere aderisce alla severa filosofia del servizio con guanti bianchi, abbinandolo alla calda ospitalità dove attenzioni personalizzate sono la regola, così come il butler in servizio 24 ore su 24 per assicurare che l'ospite debba soltanto alzare la mano, per far addirittura pulire i propri occhiali da sole stando comodamente sdraiato sul bordo della piscina. Nell'Amanjena Resort in Marocco, dove per ogni ospite sono a disposizione cinque impiegati, ogni membro dello staff è addestrato per salutare l'ospite con il proprio nome e per ricordare pure le sue preferenze personali. Per coloro che ricercano il miglioramento personale, tutti questi centri offrono un servizio personalizzato con terapeuti addestrati in particolar modo per percepire quali possano essere i bisogni ed i desideri dell'ospite.

In tutti questi Spa, l'ospite è tenuto a lasciare il pda a casa, permettendo al concierge in servizio pieno di organizzare la giornata. Tutto è possibile. Una persona disperatamente romantica al The Western Cape può ricevere un massaggio per due, arrangiato su un balcone privato con la vista sulle bellezze naturali di una Riserva naturale. All'One&Only Le Touessrok l'ospite può ricevere trattamenti Thalasso all'esterno mentre sta immerso nell'incenso di fiori e piante aromatiche provenienti dai vicini giardini esotici oppure sulla spiaggia del The Como Shambhala Spa sulle Maldive, ascoltando il soave ritmo delle onde del mare.

Questi centri di ritiro per curare salute e bellezza offrono più di una sola vacanza o la pelle abbronzata dal sole Mediterraneo o un minore golf handicap. Si tratta invece di una fuga verso un ambiente profondamente rilassante, per riacquistare lo splendore della gioventù e la vitalità senza confini d'età, in un angolo del paradiso. Molti dei Spa qui presentati stanno al servizio di tutta la persona, incorporando il miglioramento personale con la buona forma fisica. Dalla signora in vacanza all'El Tamarindo che chiede un impacco di fanghi curativi nell'aria fresca e ricca di ossigeno delle vicine foreste pluviali, all'atleta che vorrebbe restaurarsi fisicamente con movimenti meditativi nel luogo di nascita dello yoga all'Ananda Spa sulle montagne dell'Himalaya, la diversità dei programmi di questi Spa è espansiva per rispondere a tutti i tipi di richieste. Ogni ospite se ne andrà con il corpo e la mente in forma grazie alle caratteristiche terapeutiche offerte da ognuno dei Spa di classe internazionale presentati. La filosofia generale condivisa da ogni centro consiste nello sguardo focalizzato verso il centro interno per ritrovare la vera pace.

È difficile dire che cosa rende un tale Spa veramente eccezionale, ma qualunque elemento elusivo sia, i centri descritti in questo libro lo hanno presente. Questi luoghi di ritiro riposanti sono lussuosamente illustrati su ogni pagina, includendo un breve testo descrittivo che introduce queste mete ultramoderne dove ogni ospite si trova rinnovato.

Patrice Farameh

The Grove

Chandler's Cross, United Kingdom

Traditional country mansion caters to the metropolitan elite wanting a taste of countryside. In contrast to its stately home appearance, the interiors are ultra contemporary and decadent, with stunning chandeliers, quirky artworks, extravagant textiles, and furnishings fringed with Swarovski crystals. Sequoia Spa is housed in an old stable block and has the rare privilege to offer ESPA Ayurveda treatments, which promise to take guests to a higher plane of consciousness.

Traditionelle Landhausatmosphäre für eine städtische Elite, die Landluft atmen möchte. Im Unterschied zum repräsentativen Äußeren sind die Innenräume mit Kronleuchtern, Kunstobjekten, extravaganten Stoffen und mit Swarowski-Kristallen verzierten Einrichtungsgegenständen sehr zeitgenössisch und dekadent ausgestattet. Das Sequoia-Spa in einem alten Stallgebäude lockt mit dem seltenen Privileg einer ESPA Ayurveda-Behandlung; sie verspricht, die Gäste auf eine höhere Bewusstseinsebene zu heben.

Atmosphère de maison de campagne traditionnelle destinée à une élite urbaine souhaitant respirer l'air de la campagne. Contrairement à l'extérieur représentatif, les pièces intérieures sont dotées de manière très contemporaine et décadente de lustres fantastiques, d'objets d'art curieux, de tissus extravagants et de meubles ornés de cristal Swarowski. Le spa Sequoia, situé dans les anciens bâtiments de l'écurie, attire le visiteur et offre le rare privilège des soins ayurvédiques ESPA ; ils promettent de faire atteindre au client un niveau de conscience de soi plus élevé.

Ambiente tradicional de casa de campo para una élite urbana deseosa de respirar el aire campestre. En contraste con los representativos exteriores, la decoración interior está salpicada de fantásticas lámparas de araña, curiosas piezas de arte, tejidos extravagantes y objetos cubiertos de cristal Swarowski, de un modo contemporáneo y decadente. El spa Sequoia, está ubicado en un antiguo establo y capta la atención con su tratamiento ESPA Ayurveda que promete elevar los sentidos a los más altos niveles.

Tradizionale atmosfera da casa rurale per un'elite cittadina che desidera respirare aria di campagna. In contrasto con i pomposi esterni, gli interni sono arredati in maniera attuale e un po' decadente con splendidi lampadari, oggetti d'arte, stoffe stravaganti e cristalli di Swarowski. La spa Sequoia, situata in un'antica stalla, concede il raro privilegio dei trattamenti ayuverdici ESPA, promettendo agli ospiti il raggiungimento di un livello di coscienza più alto.

This 227-room hotel has abstract paintings, hidden sculptures in the garden, and 22 meter black mosaic indoor pool.

Das Hotel hat 227 Räume mit abstrakten Gemälden, verborgene Gartenskulpturen und einen 22 Meter Indoor-Pool mit schwarzem Mosaik zu bieten.

L'hôtel dispose de 227 pièces avec peintures abstraites, sculptures de jardin cachées et une piscine intérieure de 22 mètres en mosaïque noire.

El hotel cuenta con 227 habitaciones decoradas con pinturas abstractas, esculturas ocultas en el jardín y una piscina cubierta de 22 metros decorada con mosaicos negros.

L'hotel ha 227 stanze con dipinti astratti, sculture da giardino nascoste ed una piscina coperta di 22 metri ornata di mosaici neri.

Fast lane to Nirvana. This oasis of tranquility is only 30 minutes from London Heathrow.

Schneller Weg ins Paradies. Diese Oase der Ruhe liegt nur 30 Minuten vom Flughafen London-Heathrow entfernt.

Atteindre rapidement le paradis. Cet oasis de calme se trouve à seulement 30 minutes de l'aéroport Heathrow, à Londres.

La vía al paraíso. Un oasis de placer a tan sólo 30 minutos del aeropuerto de Heathrow, London.

Una scorciatoia per il paradiso. Quest'oasi di pace dista solo 30 minuti dall'aeroporto londinese di Heathrow.

Cowley Manor

Cowley, United Kingdom

A contemporary take on an 1885 Italianate manor built on 55 acres of spectacular woodland. The interiors include bright papier mâché statues and a black leather upholstered bar. Each room is designed with a blend of warmth and minimalism, with splashes of vibrant colors on the walls, and furnishings built from earthy, organic materials of stone, leather, and wood. The C-side spa is an exceptional piece of modernist architecture sunk into the garden with glass walls and a roof planted with lavender.

Das zeitgenössisch gestaltete Herrenhaus in einem 22 Hektar großen Waldgebiet wurde 1885 in italienisierendem Stil erbaut. Im Innern befinden sich fröhliche Figuren aus Pappmaché und eine Bar in schwarzem Leder. Jeder Raum wurde gleichzeitig warm und minimalistisch gestaltet, mit belebenden Wandfarben und einer Einrichtung aus erdverbundenen, organischen Materialien wie Stein, Leder und Holz. Das C-Side Spa ist ein außergewöhnliches Stück modernistischer Architektur: Es wurde in den Garten versenkt, hat Glaswände und ein mit Lavendel bepflanztes Dach.

Ce manoir qui a été aménagé dans un style contemporain se trouve dans une splendide contrée boisée de 22 hectares. Il a été bâti en 1885 dans un style italianisant. Vous trouverez à l'intérieur des figures joyeuses en papier mâché et un bar en cuir noir. Chaque pièce est mise en valeur par un mélange de chaleur et de minimalisme, des couleurs vives sur les murs et une installation à base de matériaux organiques et liés à la terre tels que la pierre, le cuir et le bois. Le spa C-Side est un élément extraordinaire d'architecture moderniste : il a été intégré sous le jardin, est doté de murs en verre et d'un toit sur lequel a été planté de la lavande.

Este Manor decorado de forma contemporánea e insertado en un frondoso bosque de 22 hectáreas es una construcción de estilo italianizado que data de 1885. El interior lo visten alegres figuras de cartón piedra y un bar decorado con piel negra. Cada una de las estancias representa una mezcla de calidez y minimalismo, con colores vivos en las paredes y mobiliario de materiales orgánicos tales como la piedra, la piel y la madera. El spa C-Side constituye una pieza arquitectónica modernista muy singular: una construcción sumergida en el jardín, con paredes de cristal y un tejado recubierto de lavanda.

Questo moderno maniero con 22 ettari di magnifico bosco fu costruito nel 1885 in stile italianizzante. All'interno si trovano allegre figure di cartapesta ed un bar arredato in pelle nera. Ogni sala è una combinazione di calore e minimalismo, con vivaci tocchi di colore alle pareti ed un arredamento in cui prevalgono materiali naturali e legati alla terra, come la pietra, la pelle ed il legno. La spa C-Side è uno straordinario pezzo di architettura modernistica: interrata nel giardino, e provvista di pareti di vetro e di un tetto fiorito di lavanda.

This chic rural retreat has sweeping views of an extravagant Victorian cascade and four lakes.

Von diesem schicken, ländlichen Rückzugsort eröffnen sich weite Blicke über eine extravagante viktorianische Kaskade und vier Seen.

Ce lieu de retraite chic et champêtre offre un panorama fantastique sur une cascade victorienne sensationnelle et quatre lacs.

Desde este elegante y campestre rincón de recogimiento la vista alcanza una vasta panorámica sobre una extravagante cascada victoriana y cuatro lagos.

Da questo elegante rifugio di campagna si gode la vista di una particolarissima cascata artificiale di epoca vittoriana e di quattro laghi.

All 30 rooms have sleek bathrooms with a rain shower enclosed by opaque aqua-blue glass screens and deep baths.

Alle 30 Räume verfügen über elegante Bäder mit tiefen Badewannen; die Duschen sind von wasserblauen, undurch-sichtigen Glasscheiben eingerahmt.

Les 30 pièces disposent de salles de bain élégantes avec des baignoires profondes ; les douches sont encadrées de vitres opaques en verre bleu marin.

Las 30 habitaciones disponen de refinados cuartos de baño con bañera alta y una ducha enmarcada en láminas no transparentes de azul cristalino.

Le 30 stanze dispongono tutte di bei bagni con vasche profonde; le docce sono incorniciate da vetrate azzurre opache.

Whatley Manor

Easton Grey, United Kingdom

The essence of an English country house hotel, but with a modern, contemporary touch. This manor is located in the Cotswolds, in the south of England. With only 15 rooms and eight suites, guests can linger in 26 distinctively designed gardens. The spacious feel also continues in the interior: an expansive hall with a magnificent open fire; a spa, deliberately kept in European style, with the Wave-Dream-Sensory Room, which lets you float into weightlessness and timelessness.

Die Essenz eines englischen Countryhouse-Hotels, aber mit einem modernen, zeitgemäßen Touch bietet das in den südenglischen Cotswolds gelegene Herrenhaus. In 26 unterschiedlich gestalteten Gärten können die Gäste der nur 15 Zimmer und acht Suiten verweilen. Eine Großzügigkeit, die auch im Inneren ihre Entsprechung findet: in der weiten Halle mit dem mächtigen offenen Kamin, dem bewusst im europäischen Stil gehaltenen Spa mit dem Wave-Dream-Sensory-Raum, der einen in Schwere- und Zeitlosigkeit entschweben lässt.

Situé dans les Cotswolds du Sud de l'Angleterre, cet hôtel particulier offre l'essence d'une maison de campagne anglaise, accompagnée d'une touche moderne et contemporaine. Les visiteurs résidant dans les huit suites et les chambres, au nombre de 15 seulement, peuvent se reposer dans 26 jardins qui ont été chacun aménagés différemment. Ce caractère généreux trouve également son pendant à l'intérieur avec la grande salle dotée d'une imposante cheminée ouverte et le spa dont le style européen a été volontairement conservé avec sa pièce Wave-Dream-Sensory dans laquelle vous ressentirez une sensation d'apesanteur et d'intemporalité.

Esta casa señorial ubicada en los Cotswolds al sur de Inglaterra encarna la esencia de un hotel Countryhouse, pero con un toque moderno adaptado a la actualidad. Tan sólo 15 habitaciones, ocho suites y 26 jardines, todos ellos diferentes, que invitan a los huéspedes simplemente a dejar pasar el tiempo. Este derroche de generosidad se refleja igualmente en los interiores: un amplio pabellón con una imponente chimenea y un spa con la sala Wave-Dream-Sensory, expresamente concebida en estilo europeo, que emanan intemporalidad e ingravidez.

Questa casa padronale situata a Cotswold, nell'Inghilterra meridionale, possiede l'essenza di un hotel inglese in stile rurale dotato però di un tocco moderno ed attuale. Gli ospiti delle 15 camere e delle otto suite possono intrattenersi in 26 giardini, tutti diversi l'uno dall'altro. La spaziosità si rispecchia anche negli interni: nella vasta hall, impreziosita dal sontuoso camino aperto, o nella spa – mantenuta intenzionalmente in stile europeo – e provvista di una sala Wave-Dream-Sensory, per permettere alla mente di scivolare in uno spazio senza gravità e senza tempo.

In the hydrotherapy pool of the Aquarius Spa, relax and enjoy the view of Wiltshire's gentle countryside.

Im Hydrotherapie-Pool des Aquarias-Spa liegen und in die sanfte Landschaft Wiltshires schauen.

S'allonger dans la piscine d'hydrothérapie du spa Aquarias et profiter du paysage reposant du Wiltshire.

Relajarse en la piscina de hidroterapia del spa Aquarias con el suave paisaje de Wiltshire ante la vista.

Riposare nella piscina idroterapica della spa Aquarias guardando il dolce paesaggio dello Wiltshire.

Each of the comfortable and elegant rooms is individually furnished with an interior mix of antiques and modern items.

Jedes der komfortablen und eleganten Zimmer ist individuell in einem Interieur-Mix aus Antiquitäten und neuen Stücken eingerichtet.

L'intérieur de chaque chambre, confortable et élégant, a été doté d'un mélange individualisé d'antiquités et d'œuvres contemporaines.

Los interiores de las confortables y elegantes habitaciones están diseñados de forma individualizada, integrando antigüedades y objetos nuevos.

Un armonioso insieme di pezzi d'antiquariato e mobili moderni dà un tocco individuale all'arredamento delle confortevoli ed eleganti camere.

Choupana Hills

Madeira, Portugal

Set 1,600 feet up in the mountains, amidst lush, sub-tropical gardens, the resort is built in a blend of Asian and African styles. From the main building with restaurant, lobby and spa, as well as 34 colorful villas, which are built on stilts into the hillside, a magnificent view overlooks the island's capital city, Funchal, and the dark expanse of the Atlantic Ocean. The spa treatments are influenced by Africa's culture and are a subtle reference to Portugal's colonial history.

500 Meter hoch in den Bergen, inmitten üppiger subtropischer Gärten liegt das in einem asiatisch-afrikanischen Stilmix gebaute Resort. Vom Hauptgebäude mit Restaurant, Lobby und Spa wie auch von den 34 farbigen, auf Stelzen in den Hang gebauten Villen eröffnet sich ein grandioser Blick auf die Inselhauptstadt Funchal und die dunklen Weiten des Atlantiks. Die Spa-Behandlungen sind beeinflusst von der Kultur Afrikas und spielen damit auf die Kolonialgeschichte Portugals an.

C'est à 500 mètres d'altitude dans les montagnes, au milieu de jardins subtropicaux luxuriants, que se trouve l'hôtel, construit dans un mélange de style asiatique et de style africain. Le bâtiment principal comprenant restaurant, lobby et spa, ainsi que les 34 villas colorées construites sur pilotis sur le versant, offrent une vue grandiose sur Funchal, la capitale de l'île, et sur les étendues sombres de l'Atlantique. Les soins procurés dans le spa sont inspirés de la culture africaine, faisant ainsi allusion à l'histoire coloniale du Portugal.

A 500 metros de altura en las montañas, rodeado de un exuberante jardín subtropical, se ubica un resort con una construcción que fusiona los estilos asiático y africano. Tanto desde el edificio principal, que alberga restaurante, spa y vestíbulo, como desde cualquiera de las 34 coloridas villas construidas sobre pilotes en la ladera, se abren unas vistas grandiosas a la capital de la isla, Funchal, y a la profunda vastedad del Atlántico. Los tratamientos que ofrece el spa se basan en influencias africanas, denotando la historia colonial de Portugal.

Il resort, costruito in stile misto asiatico-africano, sorge a 500 metri di altitudine, nel mezzo di un rigoglioso giardino subtropicale. Sia dall'edificio principale con ristorante, lobby e spa, sia dalle 34 ville, costruite sul pendio, si gode di una vista mozzafiato su Funchal, la capitale dell'isola, e sulle oscure vastità dell'Atlantico. I trattamenti della spa risentono dell'influsso della cultura africana e ricordano il passato coloniale del Portogallo.

Warm earthy tones and craftsmanship from Africa and Madeira define the ambiance in the lobby.

Warme erdige Töne und Kunsthandwerk aus Afrika und Madeira bestimmen das Ambiente der Lobby.

Les tons de terre chauds et les pièces artisanales d'Afrique et de Madère définissent l'ambiance du lobby.

Los cálidos tonos ocre y las artesanías de África y Madeira crean el ambiente del vestíbulo.

I caldi colori della terra e l'artigianato africano e locale caratterizzano l'atmosfera della lobby.

Hamam, **rasul** *bath and an indoor pool invite guests to relax.*

Hamam, Rasulbad *und ein Indoorpool laden zur Entspannung ein.*

Le hammam, *le bain Rasul et une piscine couverte invitent à la détente.*

El Hamam, *el baño Rasul y la piscina cubierta llaman al relax.*

Hamam, bagno *Rasul e piscina coperta invitano al relax.*

La Réserve Genève Hotel and Spa

Geneva, Switzerland

Star designer Jaques Garcia takes guests in the hotel's 102 unusual rooms on a "static journey". The setting amidst a green country park on the eastern bank of Lake Geneva and the interplay of vegetation and water inspired him to his idea of designing the lobby-lounge in the style of an African safari lodge: heavy, brown leather arm-chairs, brightly colored parrots, old leather suitcases and an elephant presiding majestically above it all. In contrast, the 6,500 square foot spa is kept entirely in cream-white.

Auf eine „immobile Reise" nimmt Stardesigner Jaques Garcia die Gäste des ungewöhnlichen 102-Zimmer-Hotels mit. Die Lage inmitten eines grünen Landschaftspark am Ostufer des Genfer Sees, das Zusammenspiel von Vegetation und Wasser inspirierte ihn zu seiner Idee, die Lobby-Lounge wie eine afrikanische Safari-Lodge zu gestal-ten: schwere braune Ledersessel, knallbunte Papageien, alte Lederkoffer und über allem thront ein Elefant. Im Kontrast dazu ist der 2000 Quadratmeter große Spa ganz in Cremeweiß gehalten.

Le célèbre designer Jaques Garcia invite les visiteurs de cet hôtel insolite de 102 chambres à un « voyage immobile ». Son emplacement au milieu d'un parc naturel vert sur la rive orientale du lac de Genève et le jeu de la végétation et de l'eau lui donnèrent l'idée d'aménager le lobby-salon en safari-lodge africain : fauteuils de cuir marrons et imposants, perroquets aux couleurs vives, vieilles valises en cuir. Un éléphant trône au-dessus du tout. Le spa de 2000 mètres carrés a été entièrement conservé en blanc crème en vue de réaliser un contraste.

El diseñador de Jaques Garcia invita a un "viaje quieto" a los huéspedes de este atípico hotel con 102 habitaciones. La ubicación en medio de un parque de paisaje verde situado en la cara este del Lago Lemán y el juego de vegetación y agua han sido fuente de inspiración para el diseñador, que ideó el lounge del vestíbulo como un Safari Lodge africano. Los masivos sofás marrones de piel, papagayos multicolores y un elefante dominando la escena contrastan abiertamente con el spa de 2000 metros cua-drados, todo él en color crema.

Jaques Garcia, designer d'eccezione, ha realizzato una sorta di "viaggio immobile" per gli ospiti delle 102 camere di questo insolito hotel. La posizione, al centro di un verde parco sulla riva orientale del lago di Ginevra, con i suoi giochi di vegetazione e d'acqua, gli ha ispirato l'idea di realizzare la Lobby Lounge nello stile di un Safari Lodge africano: pesanti poltrone di pelle marrone, pappagalli variopinti, vecchie valigie di pelle e perfino un elefante che troneggia sul tutto. La spa invece, che copre una superficie di 2000 metri quadrati, è realizzata in color crema.

82 feet is the length of the violet indoor pool. From the swimming pool in the hotel's private parkland, guests overlook Lake Geneva.

25 Meter lang ist das violette Hallenbad. Vom Schwimmbad in der ho-teleigenen Parkanlage aus hat man einen Blick auf den Genfer See.

La piscine couverte violette fait 25 mètres de long. La piscine située dans le parc appartenant à l'hôtel offre aux visiteurs une vue sur le lac de Genève.

La piscina cubierta de color violeta alcanza 25 metros. Desde la piscina del parque privado se disfruta de las vistas al Lago Lemán.

La piscina, di colore viola, è lunga 25 metri. Dalle vasche, nel parco dell'hotel, si può ammirare il lago di Ginevra.

In the Spa with the promising name of *Une autre histoire*, guests can enjoy slimming massages with creams made from Brazilian coffee.

Im Spa mit dem verheißungsvollen Namen *Une autre histoire* werden Schlankheitsmassagen mit Cremes aus brasilianischem Kaffee verabreicht.

Dans ce spa au nom prometteur, *Une autre histoire*, des massages amincissants sont effectués à la crème de cafés brésiliens.

El spa, con el esperanzador nombre *Une autre histoire*, propone masajes adelgazantes a base de cremas enriquecidas con café de Brasil.

Nella spa, dal promettente nome *Une autre histoire*, si praticano massaggi snellenti con creme a base di caffè brasiliano.

Victoria-Jungfrau
Grand Hotel & Spa

Interlaken, Switzerland

For years, the Grand Hotel, set at the foot of the majestic constellation of Jungfrau, Eiger and Mönch, has succeeded in maintaining its top rank in the Swiss luxury hotel trade. The secret is consistently surprising loyal and longstanding guests with new ideas. The latest coup: the ESPA, integrated into your own, private space, including Asian-inspired and generous spa suites.

Seit Jahren kann das am Fuß des erhabenen Dreigestirns Jungfrau, Eiger und Mönch gelegene Grandhotel seine Spitzenstellung in der Schweizer Luxushotellerie behaupten. Nicht zuletzt, weil man auch langjährige Stammgäste mit immer neuen Ideen zu überraschen vermag. Letzter Coup: der in einem eigenen, privat gehaltenen Bereich gebaute ESPA und die dazugehörenden, asiatisch inspirierten großzügigen Spa-Suiten.

Depuis des années, le grand-hôtel, placé au pied de la superbe triade Jungfrau, Eiger et Mönch, affirme sa position de leader dans l'hôtellerie de luxe suisse, notamment grâce à des idées nouvelles lui permettant de réserver régulièrement des surprises, même à ses clients fidèles de longue date. La dernière en date : le ESPA, construit dans une zone indépendante et respectant le domaine privé, ainsi que les suites attenantes et généreuses du spa, inspirées du style asiatique.

A los pies de los míticos picos Jungfrau, Eiger y Mönch el Grandhotel se jacta desde hace años de su puesto privilegiado en la hostelería suiza de lujo. Y ello se debe en gran medida a su constante capacidad para sorprender a los huéspedes ya habituales con nuevas ideas. La más reciente: el ESPA ubicado en un espacio propio privado y sus amplias Spa-suites de inspiración asiática.

Questo Grand Hotel, adagiato ai piedi delle tre maestose vette della Jungfrau, dell'Eiger e del Mönch, vanta da anni il primato tra gli hotel di lusso svizzeri. Ciò è dovuto anche alla capacità d riuscire a stupire perfino gli habitué con idee sempre nuove. L'ultima sorpresa: l'ESPA costruita in un'area privata propria con spaziose suite arredate in stile orientale.

Turn-of-the-century opulence meets present-day: the swimming pool, designed in Roman style, is the centerpiece of the spa area.

Jahrhundertwendeglanz trifft auf Gegenwart: Kernstück des Wellnessbereich ist die nach römischem Vorbild gestaltete Schwimmhalle.

La rencontre de la splendeur de la fin du siècle avec le présent : la partie essentielle de la zone wellness est la piscine, aménagée selon le modèle romain.

El resplandor de fin de siglo se encuentra con el presente: el pabellón de la piscina, construido según el modelo romano, constituye el núcleo del espacio wellness.

Fascino di fine secolo e presente si incontrano: la piscina, realizzata secondo il modello romano, rappresenta il nucleo dell'area wellness.

Like the deck of a modern luxury cruise-liner—this is the design of the reception area in the ESPA and it creates a delightful contrast to the playful charm of the original building.

Wie das Deck eines modernen Luxusliners ist der Empfangsbereich im ESPA gestaltet und bietet damit einen reizvollen Kontrast zum spielerischen Charme des ursprünglichen Gebäudes.

La zone de réception du ESPA est aménagée comme le pont d'un navire de ligne de luxe moderne, offrant ainsi un superbe contraste par rapport au charme désinvolte du bâtiment d'origine.

El vestíbulo del ESPA está concebido como la cubierta de un moderno crucero creando un atractivo contraste con el gracioso encanto del edificio original.

La reception dell'ESPA è concepita come la coperta di un moderno aereo di lusso in delizioso contrasto con il fascino giocoso dell'edificio originale.

Bulgari Hotels & Resorts Milano

Milan, Italy

The design metropolis of Milan is the choice of exclusive jeweler, Bulgari, for the location of his first hotel. Within walking distance of Milan's La Scala in the historic quarter of Brera and nestling in a 13,000-square foot garden, the luxury hotel perfectly reflects the philosophy of this exclusive brand. Only heavy and precious materials were used: black marble from Zimbabwe, bronze and gold mosaics for the indoor pool. In the spa, a special lighting effect ensures an especially relaxing atmosphere.

Die Design-Metropole Mailand hat sich der Nobel-Juwelier Bulgari zum Standort für sein erstes Hotel erkoren. In Gehweite zur Mailänder Scala im historischen Stadtteil Brera, eingebettet in einen 4000 Quadratmeter großen Garten, spiegelt das Luxushotel perfekt die Philosophie des Nobel-Labels wieder. Verarbeitet wurden nur schwere, kostbarste Materialien: schwarzer Marmor aus Simbabwe, Bronze, Goldmosaiken für den Innenpool. Im Spa sorgt eine spezielle Lichttechnik für eine besonders entspannende Atmosphäre.

Pour son premier hôtel, le bijoutier de luxe Bulgari a choisi Milan, métropole du design. A quelques minutes de marche de la Scala de Milan dans le quartier historique de la ville Brera, intégré dans un jardin de 4000 mètres carrés, l'hôtel de luxe reflète parfaitement la philosophie de la marque de luxe. Seuls des matériaux imposants et extrêmement précieux ont été retenus : marbre noir du Zimbabwe, bronze, mosaïques en or pour la piscine intérieure. Dans le spa, une technique de lumière spéciale crée une atmosphère particulièrement reposante.

El joyero de élite Bulgari ha escogido Milán, la metrópoli del diseño, para albergar a su primer hotel. La filosofía de la prestigiosa marca se ve reflejada a la perfección en este hotel de lujo inmerso en 4000 metros cuadrados de jardín y ubicado en el barrio histórico de Brera, a distancia a pie del teatro de la Scala. El interior lo componen materiales pesados y costosos: mármol negro de Zimbabue, bronce y mosaicos de oro en la piscina cubierta. El spa cuenta con una técnica especial de iluminación destinada a proporcionar un exclusivo ambiente de relax.

Il creatore di gioielli di lusso, Bulgari, ha scelto Milano, la metropoli del design, come sede del suo primo hotel. A pochissima distanza dalla Scala, situato nello storico quartiere di Brera, nel mezzo di un parco di 4000 metri quadrati, questo lussuoso hotel rispecchia perfettamente la filosofia del prestigioso marchio. Per costruirlo sono stati utilizzati soltanto i materiali più solidi e più preziosi: marmo nero dello Zimbabwe, bronzo, mosaici d'oro per la piscina interna. Una speciale tecnica d'illuminazione crea nella spa un'atmosfera particolarmente rilassante.

Black dominating marble and clear lines create a contemporary, luxurious ambiance in the lobby.

Schwarzer dominanter Marmor und klare Linienführung kreieren ein zeitgemäßes, luxuriöses Ambiente in der Lobby.

Le marbre noir dominant et les contours précis créent une ambiance contemporaine et luxurieuse dans le lobby.

El penetrante mármol negro y la claridad de líneas envuelven al vestíbulo de una atmósfera actual y lujosa.

Marmo nero come materiale dominante e contorni ben definiti creano nella lobby un ambiente lussuoso e moderno.

 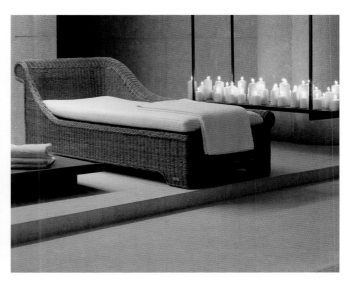

Reduction and elegance enter into a congenial relationship.

Reduktion und Eleganz gehen eine kongeniale Verbindung ein.

L'alliance de la réduction et de l'élégance offre un résultat fabuleux.

Minimalismo y elegancia se fusionan en perfección pura.

Essenzialità ed eleganza in perfetta sintonia.

Kempinski Hotel Nikopolis

Thessaloniki, Greece

A dramatic and daring reinvention of the urban resort for the savvy traveler, located in the port-city of Thessaloniki, the second capital of Greece. The architectural design is a brilliant collision of influences, with splashes of bold colors throughout the interiors of this ultra contemporary resort. The hotel's 99 rooms are grouped in joined pavilions around the largest outdoor pool in the region in a series of low-rise buildings covering 65,000 square-feet of landscaped gardens and palm trees.

Eine dramatische und kühne Neuerfindung eines städtischen Resorts für den versierten Reisenden in der Hafenstadt Thessaloniki, der zweiten Hauptstadt Griechenlands. Die Architektur vereint auf brillante Weise verschiedene Einflüsse, kräftige Farben bestimmen das Innere dieses zeitgenössischen Hotels. Die 99 Räume des Hotels gruppieren sich in untereinander verbundenen Pavillons um den größten Außenpool der Region. Die niedrigen Gebäude liegen inmitten eines 20 000 Quadratmeter großen, mit Palmen bestandenen Landschaftsgartens.

La redécouverte dramatique et audacieuse d'un complexe urbain pour le voyageur chevronné dans la ville portuaire de Thessaloniki, la seconde capitale de la Grèce. L'architecture réunit brillamment diverses influences, la totalité de l'intérieur de cet hôtel contemporain est rehaussée par des touches de couleurs. Les 99 pièces de cet hôtel sont regroupées en pavillons reliés les uns aux autres autour de la plus grande piscine extérieure de la région. Les bâtiments peu élevés sont situés au centre d'un jardin paysager de 20 000 mètres carrés composé de palmiers.

Para el viajero entendido se trata del descubrimiento dramático y atrevido de un refugio dentro de la ciudad portuaria Thessaloniki, la segunda capital de Grecia. La arquitectura aúna de forma brillante influencias de diverso carácter. En todos los rincones de este hotel extremadamente contemporáneo brilla el colorido. Las 99 habitaciones están agrupadas en pabellones comunicados entre sí, entorno a la piscina descubierta más grande de la región. Los edificios bajos se encuentran en medio de un jardín de palmeras de 20 000 metros cuadrados.

Una re-invenzione singolare ed audace di un rifugio cittadino per viaggiatori appassionati situata nel porto di Salonicco, la seconda città della Grecia. L'architettura unisce felicemente influssi differenti colori vivaci caratterizzano gli interni di questo hotel supermoderno. Le 99 sale sono raggruppate in padiglioni collegati tra loro intorno alla più grande piscina aperta della regione. I bassi edifici sono situati in mezzo ad un palmeto di 20 000 metri quadrati.

The interiors have a theatrical mixture of the modern, the postmodern, and even eccentric surrealism.

Die Innenräume bieten eine theatralische Mixtur aus Moderne, Postmoderne und sogar exzentrischem Surrealismus.

Les pièces intérieures offrent un mélange théâtral de moderne, de postmoderne et même de surréalisme excentrique.

Los espacios interiores presentan una teatral mixtura de modernidad, postmodernidad e incluso surrealismo excéntrico.

Gli interni presentano una teatrale combinazione di eccentrico surrealismo moderno e postmoderno.

Kempinski Hotel Barbaros Bay

Bodrum, Turkey

This luxurious hotel 8.7 miles from the sailing resort of Bodrum is set within large verdant gardens and a few steps from a long sandy beach. The Six Senses Spa is Turkey's largest, covering some 59 000 square feet. The Spa provides guests a modern mix of traditional regional treatments like the famed Turkish bath hamam fused with Asian spa philosophy.

Dieses Luxushotel inmitten von üppigen Gärten liegt 14 Kilometer vom Yachthafen von Bodrum und nur wenige Schritte von einem langen Sandstrand entfernt. Mit 5500 Quadratmeter ist der Six Senses Spa der größte der Türkei. Er verwöhnt seine Gäste mit einer modernen Synthese aus traditionellem türkischen Bad – dem Hamam – und asiatischer Spa-Philosophie.

Cet hôtel de luxe situé au milieu de jardins luxuriants se trouve à 14 kilometrès du port de yachts de Bodrum et à quelques pas seulement d'une longue plage de sable. Il est le plus grand spa Six Senses de Turquie avec ses 5500 mètres carrés. Ses visiteurs découvriront une synthèse moderne du bain turc traditionnel (le hammam) et de la philosophie asiatique du spa.

Este hotel de lujo insertado en un jardín opulento se encuentra a sólo 14 kilómetros del puerto deportivo de Bodrum y a unos pocos pasos de una extensa playa de arena. Con sus 5500 metros cuadrados, el spa Six Senses se ha convertido en el mayor de Turquía y deleita a sus huéspedes con una fusión moderna del baño tradicional hamam y de la filosofía asiática del spa.

Questo hotel di lusso che sorge nel mezzo di un rigoglioso giardino si trova a 14 chilometri dal porticciolo di Bodrum, in cui sono ormeggiati gli yacht, e soltanto a pochi passi da una lunga spiaggia sabbiosa. La Six Senses Spa è, con i suoi 5500 metri quadrati, la più grande della Turchia. Gli ospiti vengono viziati con una moderna sintesi tra il bagno turco – l'hamam – e la filosofia spa asiatica.

A breathtaking seaside infinity pool overlooks the Aegean Sea.

Ein atemberaubender Infinity-Pool überblickt das Ägäische Meer.

Au bord de la mer, une piscine panoramique sensationnelle offre une superbe vue sur la mer Égée.

Una Infinity Pool se funde con el mar abriéndose a la espectacular vista sobre el Mar Egeo.

Una spettacolare infinity pool si affaccia sul Mar Egeo.

Each of the 173 rooms and suites has panoramic views over its own crystal blue bay.

Aus jedem der 173 Zimmer und Suiten eröffnen sich Panoramablicke über die eigene, kristallblaue Bucht.

Les 173 chambres et suites offrent chacune une superbe vue sur la baie attenante en bleu cristal.

Desde cualquiera de las 173 habitaciones y suites se disfruta la panorámica a la bahía propia de un azul cristalino.

Tutte le 173 camere e suite si affacciano sulla baia privata, di un azzurro intenso.

Kempinski Hotel Barbaros Bay   *Bodrum, Turkey*   53

Amanjena

Marrakech, Morocco

13 acre desert sanctuary is walled and colonnaded for absolute privacy, and set in a secluded oasis of date palms and olive groves, manicured gardens of lush plants, original turquoise lagoons, and discreet corridors of meticulous tile work. Its distinctive Moorish style is modestly contemporary, yet authentic and harmoniously integrated with the Moroccan culture. With only 40 generously sized guest rooms and over 200 employees, each guest is assured a personal, memorable experience.

Die 5 Hektar große Zuflucht in der Wüste bietet dank Mauern und Kolonnaden absolute Privatheit. Das Hotel in einer abgeschiedenen Oase mit Dattelpalmen und Olivenhainen lockt mit gepflegten, üppigen Gärten, türkisfarbenen Lagunen und gefliesten Korridoren. Sein ausgeprägt maurischer Stil ist angenehm zeitgenössisch aber dennoch authentisch und fügt sich harmonisch in die marokkanische Tradition ein. Mit nur 40 großzügig geschnittenen Zimmern und über 200 Angestellten schenkt es jedem Gast eine persönliche und unvergessliche Erfahrung.

Le refuge de 5 hectares situé dans le désert offre un caractère privé absolu grâce à ses murs et à ses colonnades. L'hôtel situé dans un oasis isolé avec dattiers et oliveraie attire le visiteur avec ses jardins entretenus et luxuriants, ses lagunes turquoise et ses couloirs carrelés. Le style maure prononcé est agréablement contemporain, mais toutefois authentique, et s'intègre de manière harmonieuse à la tradition marocaine. Avec seulement 40 chambres disposant d'une surface importante et plus de 200 employés, il offre à chaque visiteur une expérience personnelle et inoubliable.

Un refugio de 5 hectáreas en el desierto rodeado por murallas y columnatas que garantizan privacidad absoluta. Ubicado en un oasis apartado rodeado de palmeras datileras y olivos, el hotel cautiva con su cuidado y opulento jardín, lagunas turquesa y pasillos de pulidos azulejos. El lugar emana un estilo árabe contemporáneo sin por ello perder autenticidad y en plena armonía con la tradición marroquí. Sólo 40 amplias habitaciones y más de 200 personas de servicio que permiten a los huéspedes vivir un derroche de atención personal.

Questo rifugio nel deserto, che si estende su una superficie di 5 ettari giornate, offre privacy completa, grazie alle mura ed ai colonnati. L'hotel, situato in un'oasi appartata circondata da palme da dattero e da ulivi, incanta con giardini curati e rigogliosi, lagune turchine e passerelle finemente piastrellate. Lo stile, dai forti influssi moreschi, è piacevolmente moderno e tuttavia autentico, e si inserisce armonicamente nella tradizione marocchina. L'hotel, che dispone di sole 40 spaziose camere ed ha più di 200 dipendenti, regala ad ogni ospite un'esperienza personale indimenticabile.

Architect *Ed Tuttle reinvented the mosque architecture bringing a nomadic feel to Islamic design.*

Der Architekt *Ed Tuttle hat die Architektur der Moscheen neu erfunden und das islamische Design um ein nomadisches Flair bereichert.*

L'architecte *Ed Tuttle a réinventé l'architecture des mosquées et enrichi le design islamique d'un flair nomade.*

El arquitecto *Ed Tuttle ha reinventado la arquitectura de las mezquitas y el diseño árabe con objeto de crear una atmósfera nómada.*

L'architetto *Ed Tuttle ha rivisitato l'architettura delle moschee ed ha arricchito di fascino nomade il design islamico.*

An enormous man-made reflection pool is the central water basin. Open-plan bathrooms with green Ouarzazate marble highlight the garden setting.

Ein enormer künstlicher Spiegelteich bildet das zentrale Schwimmbecken. Offene Baderäume mit grünem Marmor aus Ouarzazat fügen sich in die Gartenanlage ein.

L'énorme étang-miroir artificiel crée la piscine centrale. Les espaces de bain en plein air en marbre vert de Ouarzazat se fondent dans les jardins.

Un enorme estanque artificial forma la piscina central. Las estancias para baños recubiertas de mármol verde de Ouarzazat se funden en el Jardín.

La piscina centrale è costituita da un grandissimo specchio d'acqua artificiale. I bagni a vista, in marmo verde di Ouarzazat, formano un tutt'uno con i giardini.

Al Maha Desert Resort & Spa

Dubai, United Arab Emirates

A more spectacular setting is impossible: in the apparently never-ending stretch of Arabian Desert, amidst a 87-square mile nature reserve is the luxury resort, built in the style of a Bedouin camp. In the Jumilah Spa, which resembles a green oasis with waterfalls and palms, guests enjoy treatments based on centuries of Arabian traditions and knowledge of the healing power of dates and incense.

Spektakulärer könnte die Lage nicht sein: In der unendlich scheinenden Weite der arabischen Wüste, inmitten eines 225 Quadratkilometer umfassenden Naturreservats befindet sich das wie ein Beduinencamp gebaute Luxusresort. Im Jumilah-Spa, der einer grünen Oase mit Wasserfällen und Palmen gleicht, werden Anwendungen verabreicht, die auf jahrhundertealten arabischen Traditionen und dem Wissen um die Heilkraft von Datteln und Weihrauch beruhen.

Il aurait été difficile de trouver un emplacement plus spectaculaire: c'est dans l'étendue apparemment infinie du désert arabe, au milieu d'une réserve naturelle de 225 kilomètres carrés, que se trouve l'hôtel de luxe, semblable à un camp de bédouins. Dans le spa Jumilah, pareil à un oasis vert avec chutes d'eau et palmiers, les clients peuvent obtenir des soins reposant sur des traditions arabes vieilles de plusieurs siècles et sur la connaissance de la vertu curative des dattes et de l'encens.

No existe ubicación más espectacular. El resort de lujo concebido como un campamento beduino está inmerso en el infinito desierto árabe, dentro de una reserva natural que abarca 225 kilómetros cuadrados. En el Jumilah Spa, un oasis verde de palmeras y cascadas, se llevan a cabo tratamientos basados en tradiciones árabes centenarias y los conocimientos sobre las propiedades del dátil y el incienso.

La posizione non potrebbe essere più spettacolare: nell'immensità infinita del deserto arabo, al centro di una riserva naturale di 225 chilometri quadrati, si trova questo resort di lusso la cui costruzione ricorda un campo di beduini. Nella spa Jumilah, simile ad una verde oasi con palme e giochi d'acqua, i trattamenti praticati si richiamano alle secolari tradizioni arabe ed all'antica sapienza che custodisce il segreto potere terapeutico dei datteri e dell'incenso.

Freshen up from the glimmering desert heat in the cooled pool.

Erfrischung von der flirrenden Wüstenhitze bietet der gekühlte Pool.

La piscine réfrigérée permet de se rafraîchir après avoir goûté à la chaleur étourdissante du désert.

El calor abrasador del desierto se vuelve frescor en la piscina.

La piscina rinfrescata: refrigerio al caldo torrido del deserto.

Architecture and color scheme correspond perfectly to the magnificent surrounding nature.

Architektur und Farbgebung korrespondieren perfekt mit der umgebenen grandiosen Natur.

L'architecture et le choix des couleurs correspondent parfaitement à la nature grandiose entourant l'hôtel.

Arquitectura y cromatismo se corresponden a la perfección con la grandiosa naturaleza del entorno.

L'architettura ed i colori si adattano splendidamente alla grandiosa natura circostante.

Madinat Jumeirah

Dubai, United Arab Emirates

An oriental city out of "Thousand and One Nights" is the style of the Madinat, located on Jumeirah Beach. The hotel consists of three different hotels and a Souk. The focal point is the palace Al Qasr, designed with opulent Arabian ornamentation. You reach the Six Senses Spa with its 26 treatment pavilions by boat, across labyrinthine waterways.

Einer orientalischen Stadt aus „Tausendundeiner Nacht" gleicht das am Jumeirah-Beach gelegene Madinat, das aus drei unterschiedlichen Hotels und einem Souk besteht. Mittelpunkt bildet der mit verschwenderischer arabischer Ornamentik gestaltete Palast Al Qasr. Das Six Senses Spa mit seinen 26 Behandlungspavillons erreicht man mit dem Boot über verschlungene Wasserwege.

Situé tout près de la Jumeirah-Beach, le complexe Madinat, composé de trois hôtels différents et d'un souk, évoque une ville orientale des « Mille et Une Nuits ». Le palace Al Qasr, décoré d'ornementations arabes à profusion, représente le point central. Le spa Six Senses, qui compte 26 pavillons destinés aux soins, est accessible par bateau en empruntant des canaux navigables serpentins.

Como una ciudad oriental de "Las mil y una noches" se levanta el Madinat, en la playa de Jumeirah, formando un complejo de tres hoteles diferentes y un zoco. El centro de atención lo crea el Al Qasr cargado de una ostentosa ornamentación árabe. El Six Senses Spa cuenta con 26 pabellones para tratamientos a los que se accede en barco a través de entramados canales.

Il complesso Madinat, situato sulla spiaggia di Jumeirah e costituito da tre diversi hotel e da un souk, somiglia ad una città orientale da "Mille e una notte". Il punto focale è costituito dal palazzo Al Qasr, riccamente decorato in stile moresco. La spa Six Senses, con i suoi 26 padiglioni per i vari trattamenti, è raggiungibile in barca su intricati corsi d'acqua.

The light-filled treatment pavilions were designed according to Feng Shui principles.

Die lichtdurchfluteten Behandlungspavillons wurden nach Feng-Shui-Gesichtspunkten gestaltet.

Baignés de lumières, les pavillons destinés aux soins ont été aménagés selon des principes Feng Shui.

Los luminosos pabellones para tratamientos han sido concebidos según los puntos faciales de Feng-Shui.

I luminosi padiglioni sono stati realizzati secondo i principi del Feng Shui.

The characteristic wind-towers and historic ornaments reflect the Arabian heritage.

Die charakteristischen Windtürme und historische Ornamente reflektieren das arabische Erbe.

Les tours à vent caractéristiques et les ornements historiques reflètent l'héritage arabe.

Los característicos minaretes y ornamentos históricos son reflejo de la herencia árabe.

Le caratteristiche torri del vento e gli ornamenti storici rispecchiano l'influsso arabo.

One&Only Royal Mirage

Dubai, United Arab Emirates

Oriental opulence radiates from the entire facility with its three different hotels in a 29-acre area, located directly on Dubai's fine-sandy Jumeirah Beach. The lobby offers an extensive vista overlooking the skillfully positioned pools and palm gardens, as far as the artificially created Palm Island and the deep blue of the Arabian Gulf. At the end of 2002 the health and beauty institute opened with the exclusive Givenchy Spa, offering classic treatments as well as hamam massages and steam baths in Arabian tradition.

Orientalische Opulenz strahlt das gesamte Anwesen aus mit seinen drei unterschiedlichen Hotels, die in einem Areal von zwölf Hektar direkt an Dubais feinsandigem Jumeirah-Beach liegen. Die Lobby bietet einen weiten Blick über kunstvoll angelegte Pools und Palmengärten hinweg auf das künstlich angelegte Palm Island und das tiefe Blau des Arabischen Golfs. Im Ende 2002 eröffneten Health and Beauty-Institut verwöhnt ein anspruchsvoller Givenchy-Spa mit klassischen Anwendungen, der Hamam bietet Massagen und Dampfbäder in arabischer Tradition.

La totalité du complexe est une expression de l'opulence orientale avec trois hôtels différents situés sur une surface de douze hectares le long de la plage de sable fin Jumeirah Beach de Dubaï. Le lobby offre une vue sublime des piscines et des jardins de palmiers conçus avec beaucoup d'art, jusqu'à l'île artificielle de Palm Island et le bleu intense du Golfe persique. Dans l'institut de beauté et de remise en forme ouvert à la fin de l'année 2002, un Givenchy Spa impressionnant procure des soins classiques, le hammam propose des massages et des bains de vapeur selon la tradition arabe.

Todo un recinto que emana opulencia árabe, a los pies de la arena fina de la playa de Jumeirah de Dubai y con tres hoteles diferentes repartidos en un espacio de doce hectáreas. El vestíbulo lanza amplias vistas que abarcan las artísticas piscinas, el jardín de palmeras, y alcanzan hasta la isla artificial de Palm Island y el azul intenso del golfo árabe. A finales de 2002 fue abierto el Health and Beauty-Institut y su exigente Givenchy Spa con tratamientos clásicos, hamam para masajes y baños de vapor en la más absoluta tradición árabe.

L'intero complesso, con i suoi tre hotel situati su un'area di dodici ettari direttamente su Jumeriah, la spiaggia di Dubai dalla sabbia finissima, irradia opulenza orientale. Dalla lobby si possono ammirare le piscine ed i palmeti, la cui vista si allunga fino a Palm Island, ricavata artificialmente, e si perde nell'azzurro intenso del Golfo Arabico. Nell'Istituto di Salute e Bellezza, aperto alla fine del 2002, l'eccellente Givenchy Spa, vizia gli ospiti con trattamenti classici, mentre l'Hamam offre massaggi e bagni turchi secondo la tradizione araba.

High-dome buildings, finely crafted arches and rich ornamentation influence the oriental ambiance in the spacious spa.

Hohe Kuppelbauten, fein ausgearbeitete Bögen und reiche Ornamentik prägen das orientalische Ambiente im weitläufigen Spa.

Les coupoles hautes, les arcs finement travaillés et l'ornementation abondante soulignent l'ambiance orientale de ce spa gigantesque.

Cúpulas elevadas, arcadas detalladamente trabajadas y una rica ornamentación envuelven al extenso spa en el ambiente oriental.

Alti edifici a cupola, archi finemente lavorati e ricche decorazioni caratterizzano l'atmosfera orientale della spaziosa spa.

In the hamam, with its various steam baths and jacuzzis, traditional Arabian massages are available.

Im Hamam mit seinen unterschiedlichen Dampfbädern und Jacuzzis werden traditionelle arabische Massagen verabreicht.

Des massages arabes traditionnels sont effectués dans le hammam, comprenant différents bains de vapeur et jacuzzis.

En el hamam, además de baños de vapor y Jacuzzi, se ofrecen masajes árabes tradicionales.

Nella Hamam con diversi bagni turchi e Jacuzzi, si praticano i tradizionali massaggi arabi.

One&Only Le Touessrok

Trou d'Eau Douce, Mauritius

A sanctuary for those demanding solitude, romance, or rejuvenation. Over 200 rooms are located either on the mainland, or as secluded suites resting on the pristine white sand beach in the adjoining privately owned island. The resort extends to other offshore islets that offer other dining experiences, activities such as golf and water sports, and the famed Givenchy Spa, where nothing is too much trouble, making it the jewel of tranquility in the middle of the sparkling neon-blue Indian Ocean.

Eine Zuflucht für alle, die Einsamkeit, Romantik oder Revitalisierung suchen. Die über 200 Zimmer liegen entweder auf dem Festland oder als abgeschlossene Suiten am unberührten, weißen Sandstrand der nahen, privaten Insel. Das Resort erstreckt sich über mehrere Eilande vor der Küste, wo man speisen oder Aktivitäten wie Golfspielen und Wassersport nachgehen kann. Nicht zu vergessen der berühmte Givenchy Spa, der keine Wünsche unerfüllt lässt – ein Juwel der Ruhe inmitten des glitzernden, neonblauen Indischen Ozeans.

Un refuge pour tous ceux qui recherchent la solitude, le romantisme ou qui souhaitent se revitaliser. Plus de 200 chambres sont situées soit sur la terre ferme, soit sous la forme suites autonomes sur la plage intacte de sable blanc de l'île privée se trouvant à proximité. Le complexe s'étend en amont de la côte sur plusieurs îlots où l'on peut dîner ou vaquer à des occupations telles que le golf ou le sport aquatique. A ne pas oublier, le célèbre spa Givenchy qui répondra à tous vos souhaits : un bijou de calme au milieu de l'océan Indien, scintillant et bleu néon.

El escondite ideal para quienes buscan, soledad, romanticismo y el poder revitalizarse. Las más de 200 habitaciones se reparten por tierra firme, o bien como suites aisladas al borde de una playa de arena blanca, como si de islas privadas se tratase. El resort se extiende por varias isletas frente a la costa dotadas de restaurantes, posibilidades para jugar al golf o practicar deportes acuáticos. Sin olvidar el famoso spa Givenchy, que concede todos los deseos en este santuario del relax en medio del brillante y profundo azul del Océano Índico.

Un rifugio per tutti coloro che cercano solitudine, romanticismo o rigenerazione. Le camere, più di 200, sono situate sulla terraferma oppure – come suite chiuse – si trovano sulla bianca spiaggia sabbiosa e intatta della vicina isola privata. Il resort si estende su più isole situate di fronte alla costa, dove si può pranzare o praticare il golf o gli sport acquatici. Da non dimenticare: la celebre Givenchy Spa, che non lascia irrealizzato nessun desiderio – un gioiello di tranquillità in mezzo al blu dello scintillante Oceano Indiano.

Soak in an egg-shaped stone tub so central, guests become a sculptural element in the room, or bathe sunny-side up on an oceanfront chaise.

Wer in diese eiförmige Steinwanne eintaucht, fühlt sich als Teil des Raumes; natürlich können Sie auch in einer Liege am Meer die Sonne genießen.

En plongeant dans cette baignoire ovoïdale en pierre, vous aurez la sensation de faire partie intégrante de la pièce ; vous pourrez évidemment profiter également du soleil dans une chaise longue au bord de la mer.

Dentro de esta bañera ovalada de piedra se tiene la sensación de ser parte integral de la sala. Si bien otra opción es disfrutar del sol en una tumbona frente al mar.

Chi si immerge in questa vasca di pietra ovale si sente parte della stanza; naturalmente, è possibile godere il sole anche sdraiati in riva al mare.

Interiors are designed with opulent materials to interpret the island's landscape and history.

Die **verschwenderisch** *ausgestatteten Innenräume verweisen auf Landschaft und Geschichte der Insel.*

Les **pièces** *intérieures décorées avec opulence évoquent le paysage et l'histoire de l'île.*

Los **interiores** *están decorados de forma suntuosa y reflejando en detalle el paisaje y la historia de la isla.*

Il **ricco** *arredamento degli interni rievoca il paesaggio e la storia dell'isola.*

The Western Cape Hotel & Spa

Hermanus, South Africa

Natural beauties surrounding Cape Town are the backdrop for this majestic estate on cascading banks bordered by the Kogelberg Nature Reserve. The architects worked closely with conservation experts to ensure that the property blends in with the natural environment and the protected biosphere reserve. At the AltiraSPA, healing and relaxation focuses on water, where visitors can immerse themselves in the Hydro-pool, or relax on one of the soothing water beds with tranquil vistas.

Die Naturschönheiten um Kapstadt bilden den Hintergrund für das majestätische Anwesen auf dem abfallenden Ufer am Rande des Kogelberg Nature Reserve. Die Architekten haben eng mit Naturschützern zusammengearbeitet, um das Hotel harmonisch in die Natur und das Schutzgebiet einzufügen. Im AltiraSPA steht das Wasser im Mittelpunkt der Heilung und Entspannung. Die Besucher können im Hydro-Pool eintauchen oder sich auf einem der entspannenden Wasserbetten die Aussicht genießen.

Les beautés naturelles dont est entouré Le Cap constituent le décor de la propriété majestueuse sur la rive descendant le long de la réserve naturelle de Kogelberg. Les architectes ont travaillé étroitement avec les protecteurs de la nature pour intégrer harmonieusement l'hôtel dans la nature et le territoire protégé. Dans le AltiraSPA, l'eau représente l'élément central de la guérison et de la relaxation. Les visiteurs peuvent plonger dans la piscine hydro ou se détendre sur l'un des lits à eau relaxants tout en profitant de la vue de rêve.

La belleza natural alrededor de Ciudad del Cabo es escenario de una suntuosa propiedad sobre el puerto escalonado, bordeando la Kogelberg Nature Reserve. Los arquitectos han trabajado intensamente con protectores de la naturaleza, con el fin de integrar el hotel en armonía con la naturaleza y la zona protegida. En el AltiraSPA el agua se convierte en la base para la relajación y los tratamientos curativos. Los huéspedes disfrutan de las fabulosas vistas sumergiéndose en la hidro-piscina o relajándose en cualquiera de las camas de agua.

Le bellezze naturali che circondano Città del Capo fanno da scenografia a questo maestoso complesso situato sulla riva che scende ai confini della Kogelberg Nature Reserve. Gli architetti hanno collaborato strettamente con gli ecologisti allo scopo di inserire armonicamente l'hotel nella natura e nel territorio di protezione. Nella AltiraSPA l'acqua è al centro della terapia e del relax. Gli ospiti possono immergersi nella piscina con idromassaggio o rilassarsi su uno dei comodi letti ad acqua e godere della vista.

The ultramodern thalassotherapy of the spa offers 18 treatment rooms with a wide variety of specialized therapies like a brine plunging pool.

Die ultramoderne Thalassotherapie des Spa wird in 18 Behandlungsräumen angeboten, in denen ein breites Angebot spezieller Therapien zur Verfügung steht, etwa ein Sole-Tauchbad.

La thalassothérapie ultramoderne du spa est effectuée dans 18 pièces destinées aux soins qui proposent un large choix de thérapies spéciales, comme par exemple l'immersion dans l'eau saline.

La ultramoderna talasoterapia se ofrece en las 18 salas para tratamientos del spa, que además propone una amplia oferta de terapias especiales de baños de inmersión en agua salada.

La modernissima talasoterapia della spa viene praticata in 18 cabine per il trattamento, nelle quali è disponibile un'ampia scelta di terapie particolari, come i bagni d'acqua salina.

All 145 deluxe rooms *feature balconies with breathtaking views of either the Bot River lagoon, the award-winning golf course, or the plunging mountain range.*

Alle 145 Luxuszimmer *haben einen Balkon mit atemberaubenden Blicken auf die Bot River Lagune, den preisgekrönten Golfplatz oder die steil abfallenden Berge.*

Les 145 *chambres de luxe ont un balcon offrant une vue à en couper le souffle sur la lagune Bot River, le terrain de golfe primé ou les montagnes en pente abrupte.*

Las 145 *habitaciones de lujo disponen de balcón con increíbles vistas a la laguna Bot River, el galardonado campo de golf y las montañas escarpadas.*

Le 145 *camere di lusso dispongono tutte di un balcone con magnifica vista sulla Bot River Lagune, il prestigioso campo da golf o le montagne scoscese.*

Oberoi Rajvilas

Jaipur, India

An opulent resort with traditional Rajasthani architecture set amidst 32 acres of lush lawns and orchids, turquoise reflection pools, decorative fountains that play watery music, pavilions and tiled courtyards. Villas are clustered around shady gardens. Attentive staff enables each guest to live in the lifestyle of Rajasthani royalty. The world-class spa incorporates the use of Ayurvedic principles of holistic health maintenance.

Ein opulentes Resort in traditioneller Rajasthan-Architektur inmitten von 13 Hektar mit üppigen Rasenflächen und Orchideen, türkisfarbenen Spiegelteichen, plätschernden Brunnen, Pavillons und gefliesten Höfen. Die Gästevillen sind locker zwischen schattigen Gärten verteilt. Aufmerksames Personal versetzt jeden Besucher in die Welt der Maharadschas. Das Spa bietet ganzheitliche Ayurveda-Heilbehandlungen.

Un complexe opulent d'architecture Rajasthan traditionnelle au milieu de 13 hectares avec des pelouses luxuriantes et des orchidées, des étangs-miroirs couleur turquoise, des fontaines décoratives au clapotis mélodieux, des pavillons et des cours carrelées. Les villas des visiteurs sont réparties entre les jardins ombragés avec suffisamment de distance les unes par rapport aux autres. Le personnel attentionné plonge chaque visiteur dans le monde des maharadjas. Le spa de classe mondiale propose des soins ayurvédiques complets.

Un opulento resort de arquitectura tradicional de Rajastán ubicado en 13 hectáreas con exuberantes praderas, orquídeas, estanques de aguas turquesas, fuentes, pabellones y patios azulejados. Las villas para huéspedes se dispersan libremente entre jardines sombreados. Un personal atento y cuidadoso se encarga de trasladar a los visitantes al mundo de los maharajás. El spa ofrece tratamientos de salud integral Ayurveda.

Un fastoso resort in stile Rajasthan tradizionale, situato su un'area di 13 ettari con floridi prati ed orchidee, specchi d'acqua turchini, fontane in cui l'acqua mormora dolcemente, padiglioni e cortili piastrellati. Le ville sono disseminate nei giardini ombrosi. Il personale, particolarmente attento, conduce gli ospiti nel mondo dei maragià. La spa di prim'ordine propone applicazioni Ayurveda per il benessere generale.

Sculptured gardens are landscaped around a 250-year-old temple floating in a lotus pond, and a traditional mansion which now houses a luxurious Ayurvedic spa.

Skulpturale Gärten umgeben einen 250 Jahre alten Tempel, der in einem Lotosteich zu schweben scheint; in dem traditionellen Herrenhaus ist ein luxuriöser Ayurveda-Spa untergebracht.

De superbes jardins aménagés entourent un temple vieux de 250 ans qui semble flotter dans un étang de lotus ; le spa ayurvédique luxueux a été aménagé dans une maison traditionnelle.

Un templo de 250 años rodeado de esculturales jardines parece flotar en un estanque de flores de loto. La mansión tradicional alberga el lujoso spa Ayurveda.

Giardini scultorei circondano un tempio vecchio 250 anni che sembra galleggiare su uno stagno di fiori di loto; nella tradizionale casa padronale si trova una lussuosa spa Ayurveda.

71 suites blend *Moghal, Hindu and Persian styles, with marble bathrooms that open onto private walled gardens.*

In den 71 Suiten *gehen Mogul-, Hindu- und persischer Stil eine gelungene Verbindung ein; die marmornen Bäder öffnen sich in private, von Mauern umgebene Gärten.*

Dans les 71 suites, *l'alliance des styles mongol, hindou et perse s'avère parfaitement réussie ; les salles de bain en marbre s'ouvrent sur des jardins privés entourés de murs.*

En las 71 suites *se funden a la perfección los estilos mogol, hindú y persa. Los baños en mármol se abren a jardines privados amurallados.*

Nelle 71 suite *sono felicemente combinati gli stili mogol, hindu e persiano; i bagni marmorei si aprono su giardini privati circondati da mura.*

Oberoi Udaivilas

Udaipur, India

This 30-acre palatial property set against the backdrop of the Aravalli Hills was designed as a Mewari Palace in the Rajasthan era. Landscaped gardens and shady court-yards, decorative fountains with cool marble, and hidden alcoves embellished with mosaics create a romantic ambience of the idealized India. A stunning and serene place, perfect for a specially designed Ayurvedic treatment in private therapy rooms overlooking the tranquil Lake Pichola to the picturesque town of Udaipur.

Das prunkvolle, 12 Hektar große, vor dem Aravalli-Gebirge gelegene, Anwesen war ursprünglich ein Mewari-Palast der Rajasthan-Ära. Landschaftsgärten und schattige Höfe, dekorative Springbrunnen mit kühlem Marmor und verborgene, mit Mosaiken verzierte Wandnischen lassen das romantische Ambiente eines idealisierten Indiens auferstehen. Dieser überwältigende und ruhige Ort ist wie geschaffen für Ayurveda. Es wird in privaten Räumen zelebriert, von denen sich Ausblicke über den Pichola-See und die pittoreske Stadt Udaipur ergeben.

Ce refuge fastueux de 12 hectares ayant pour décor les Ârâvalli était à l'origine un palais Mewari de l'ère râjasthâni. Les jardins paysagers et les cours ombragées, les fontaines décoratives en marbre froid et les alcôves dissimulées et ornées de mosaïque contribuent à créer l'ambiance romantique d'une Inde idéalisée. Ce lieu sublime et calme semble créé pour l'Ayurveda. Elle est effectuée dans les pièces privées qui offrent une vue fantastique sur le lac Pichola et la ville pittoresque d'Udaipur.

Esta suntuosa propiedad de 12 hectáreas ubicada sobre el escenario de las Aravalli Hills fue originariamente un palacio de la dinastía Merawi perteneciente a la era de Rajastán. Jardines refinados, patios sombreados, fuentes decorativas de mármol frío y alcobas escondidas y ricamente decoradas reviven el ambiente romántico de una India idealizada. En semejante lugar de fascinación y relax la terapia Ayurveda tiene su sitio ideal. Se practica en las estancias privadas con vistas al lago Pichola y a la pintoresca ciudad de Udaipur.

Questa sfarzosa tenuta, che si stende su un'area di 12 ettari con lo sfondo dei Monti Aravalli, era originariamente un palazzo Mewari risalente al periodo in cui la regio-ne faceva parte del Rajasthan. Giardini curati e cortili ombrosi, fontane ornamentali di fresco marmo ed alcove nascoste ornate di mosaici lasciano rivivere l'atmosfera romantica dell'India favolosa. Questo luogo ammaliante e tranquillo è l'ideale per una speciale terapia Ayurveda, celebrata in sale private con vista sul lago Piccola e sulla pittoresca città di Udaipur.

Interiors have intricately crafted fabrics and furnishings artfully com-bined with Western decor to create elegantly dressed rooms and luxurious marble bathrooms.

Die Innenräume bestechen durch kunstvolle Stoffe und Einrichtungs-gegenstände, die mit westlichem Dekor zu elegant ausgestatteten Räu-men und luxuriösen Marmorbädern verschmelzen.

Les pièces intérieures fascinent par leurs tissus et les objets d'aména-gement artistiques qui se fondent avec le décor occidental pour faire ap-paraître des pièces au décor élégant et des salles de bain luxueuses en marbre.

En los interiores resaltan los tejidos artísticos y objetos decorativos que se funden con un mobiliario elegante de decoración occidental y lujosos baños de mármol.

Gli interni incantano con stoffe e oggetti di gran gusto che, uniti a decorazioni di tipo occidentale, arredano elegantemente le sale e i bagni marmorei.

The architecture features huge, beautifully crafted frescoes and ornate carving, a massive central dome, inlay work, detailed interiors, and reflection pools.

Die Architektur zeichnet sich durch riesige, wunderbar gearbeitete Fresken und Schnitzereien, eine mächtige, zentrale Kuppel, Intarsien, kunstvolle Einrichtungen und Spiegelteiche aus.

L'architecture se distingue par des fresques et des sculptures sur bois géantes et merveilleusement travaillées, une coupole centrale imposante, des éléments de marqueterie, une installation mettant l'accent sur l'art et des étangs-miroirs.

La arquitectura se caracteriza por los fabulosos y enormes frescos y tallas, una cúpula central imponente, trabajos de marquetería, mobiliario artístico y estanques.

L'architettura è caratterizzata da immensi affreschi ed intagli finemente lavorati, un'imponente cupola centrale, intarsi, splendidi arredamenti e specchi d'acqua.

Ananda in the Himalayas

Uttaranchal, India

This authentic Ayurveda resort is a spiritually charged wellness retreat that resides in a magnificent palace estate. The calming blend of lush greenery, fresh mountain air and Himalayan spring water, and the luxurious therapy rooms overlooking the holy River Ganges and the mystifying Himalayas, provides the perfect environment for spiritual and physical rejuvenation. The spa is organic in every sense, using herbs sourced from the forested foothills, and flowers from the garden for facials.

Dieses authentische Ayurveda-Resort bietet spirituelle Wellness in einem prachtvollen Palast an. Die beruhigende Mischung aus üppigem Grün, frischer Bergluft und Quellwasser aus dem Himalaja sowie luxuriöse Therapieräume mit Blick auf den heiligen Ganges und den mystischen Himalaja liefern ein perfektes Umfeld für die spirituelle und körperliche Regeneration. Der Spa ist in jeder Hinsicht organisch, die verwendeten Kräuter stammen aus dem bewaldeten Vorgebirge des Himalaja und die Blumen für die Gesichtsbehandlung aus den eigenen Gärten.

Ce complexe ayurvédique authentique propose un programme wellness spirituel dans un palais somptueux. Ce mélange reposant de vert opulent, d'air frais de la montage et d'eau de source de l'Himalaya, ainsi que les pièces de thérapie luxueuses avec vue sur le Gange sacré et l'Himalaya mystique livrent un environnement parfait pour la régénération spirituelle et corporelle. Le spa est organique à tous les points de vue, les herbes utilisées proviennent des contreforts boisés de l'Himalaya et les fleurs utilisées pour les soins du visage ont été cueillies dans les propres jardins de l'hôtel.

Este resort Ayurveda auténtico ofrece un bienestar de corte espiritual con un palacio imponente como marco. La relajante mezcla entre el verde frondoso, el aire fresco de la montaña y las aguas termales del Himalaya, unida a las lujosas salas para terapias con vistas al río sagrado Ganges y el místico Himalaya constituyen el entorno ideal para la regeneración espiritual y corporal. El spa es orgánico en todos los sentidos: las hierbas que se emplean provienen de las estribaciones boscosas del Himalaya y las plantas para los tratamientos faciales se recolectan en el propio jardín.

Questo autentico resort Ayurveda offre wellness e spiritualità all'interno di un sontuoso palazzo. La rilassante combinazione di verde intenso, fresca aria di montagna e acqua sorgiva dell'Himalaya, e lussuose sale di terapia con vista sul sacro Gange ed il mistico Himalaya sono il luogo ideale per la rigenerazione fisica e spirituale. La spa è assolutamente organica, le erbe utilizzate provengono dalle montagne boscose antistanti l'Himalaya ed i fiori per i trattamenti al viso sono quelli dei giardini privati.

This sacred locale is purported to be the birthplace of yoga, Ayurveda and meditation, and overlooks the Corbett and Rajaji National Parks.

Dieser heilige Ort soll die Geburtsstätte von Yoga, Ayurveda und Meditation sein. Er grenzt an die Nationalparks Corbett und Rajaji.

Ce lieu sacré serait le lieu de naissance du yoga, de l'ayurvéda et de la méditation. Il est attenant aux parcs nationaux de Corbett et de Rajaji.

En este lugar sagrado, limitrofe de los parques nacionales de Corbett y Rajaji, se dice que nació el yoga, el Ayurveda y la meditación.

Si racconta che in questo luogo sacro siano nati lo yoga, l'ayurveda e la meditazione. Confina con i parchi nazionali di Corbett e Rajaji.

This Himalayan *sanctuary is set amidst the palace and estates of the Maharaja of Tehri Garhwal, with Raj-inspired opulent interiors.*

Das Refugium im *Himalaja wurde im Palast und den Anwesen des Maharadschas von Tehri Garhwal eingerichtet, mit opulenten, Raj-inspirierten Innenräumen.*

Ce refuge *situé dans l'Himalaya a été aménagé dans le palais et les propriétés du Maharadja de Tehri Garhwal avec d'opulentes pièces intérieures agencées selon les projets du Radja.*

El refugio *del Himalaya fue convertido en palacio y decorado para el maharajá de Tehri Garhwal, con interiores opulentos inspirados en los rajás.*

Il rifugio *nell'Himalaya è stato realizzato nel palazzo e nella proprietà del maragià di Tehri Garhwal, con interni sontuosi ispirati ai ragià.*

The interiors of the spa are rinsed with modernity, but respectfully built without disturbing the natural roll of the hills.

Die Innenräume des Spa sind modern gehalten, zeugen aber vom Respekt vor der natürlichen Hügellandschaft.

Bien que les pièces intérieures du spa aient été aménagées selon un style moderne, elles se montrent également respectueuses du paysage vallonné naturel.

En las estancias interiores del spa son modernas, si bien la construcción respeta fielmente el paisaje natural de colinas que le rodea.

Gli interni della Spa sono mantenuti in stile moderno, pur nel rispetto del paesaggio collinare naturale.

Cocoa Island

South Malé Atoll, Maldives

Complete escapism in this private island resort where serenity and luxury is found in equal measure. Simple wooden walkways built above the shallow ocean lead to 33 villas and suites built overhanging the water in the style of the traditional Maldivian Dhonis (boats). Each suite has a private veranda with steps leading down into the azure waters of the Maldivian sea. The Como Shambhala retreat is a spa on the island where wellness is nurtured in simple timber beach houses.

Die private Insel ermöglicht einen vollständigen Rückzug in ein Resort, in dem sich Ruhe und Luxus die Waage halten. Einfache Holzstege führen über den flachen Ozean zu 33 Villen und Suiten, die über dem Wasser im Stil der traditionellen Dhonis (Boote) der Malediven erbaut wurden. Zu jeder Villa gehört eine private Veranda, von der Stufen ins azurblaue Meerwasser führen. Das Como Shambhala Retreat, ein Spa auf einer Insel, hat Wellness in einfachen Strandhäusern aus Holz anzubieten.

L'île privée permet une retraite complète dans un complexe dans lequel le calme et le luxe sont équilibrés. De simples passerelles en bois conduisent au-delà de l'océan lisse vers les 33 villas et suites qui ont été construites sur l'eau dans le style des dhonis (bateaux) traditionnels maldiviens. Chaque villa possède sa véranda privée et des marches mènent jusqu'à l'eau bleu azur de la mer des Maldives. Le Como Shambhala Retreat, un spa sur l'île, propose un programme de wellness dans de simples cabines de plage en bois.

La isla privada proporciona recogimiento en un resort en el que el relax y el lujo son la razón de ser. Las 33 villas y suites están concebidas en el estilo tradicional Dhoni (barco) de las Maldivas y a ellas se accede a través de sencillas pasarelas sobre el agua poco profunda del océano. Cada villa cuenta con una terraza privada, con escalera directa al agua azul cristalina. El spa Como Shambhala Retreat está ubicado en una isla y propone tratamientos wellness en sencillas cabañas de madera sobre la playa.

L'isola privata permette di ritirarsi completamente in un resort in cui tranquillità e lusso sono in perfetta sintonia. Semplici passerelle di legno portano, sulle placide acque dell'oceano, a 33 ville e suite, costruite sull'acqua secondo lo stile delle tradizionali Dhonis (barche) delle Maldive. Ad ogni villa appartiene una veranda privata, con gradini che portano fino all'acqua azzurra delle Maldive. Il Como Shambhala Retreat, una spa situata su un'isola, offre wellness in semplici capanne di legno.

The stylish interiors of the wooden villas are cool and uncluttered, drawing their inspiration from colonial themes, yet equipped with all the modern comforts.

Die stilvollen Innenräume der hölzernen Villen sind kühl und nicht überladen. Sie atmen zwar den Geist der Kolonialzeit, sind aber mit modernstem Komfort ausgestattet.

Les pièces intérieures stylées des villas en bois sont fraîches et ne sont pas surchargées. On y retrouve certes l'esprit de l'époque coloniale, mais elles sont dotées du confort le plus moderne.

Los interiores de las villas de madera están cargados de estilo, sin excesos y con un aire de frescor. Aunque aún respiran el espíritu de la época colonial no carecen de todo el moderno confort.

I raffinati interni delle ville di legno sono freschi e discreti. Pur rievocando l'epoca coloniale, sono dotati di tutti i comfort moderni.

This private island hideaway has many hidden corners of quiet places where you can enjoy nature's power to overwhelm.

Das private Inselrefugium hat viele einsame Ecken voller Ruhe anzubieten, wo der Gast vom Natureindruck überwältigt wird.

Ce refuge insulaire privé possède de nombreux recoins déserts très calmes où le visiteur sera submergé par la nature qui l'entoure.

Esta isla de retiro cuenta con rincones cargados de tranquilidad en los que los huéspedes se dejan embriagar por el espectáculo natural.

Il rifugio privato sull'isola offre molti angoli solitari pieni di tranquillità che incantano gli ospiti con la bellezza della natura.

One&Only Maldives at Reethi Rah

North Malé Atoll, Maldives

130 villas are discreetly placed amidst beautiful landscaping on one of the largest islands in North Malé Atoll, each occupying its own secluded piece of white sand shores or private deck over crystal turquoise waters of the lagoon. Set in lush vegetation, all villas are spaced 66 feet apart for an unprecedented degree of privacy. A dedicated villa host personalizes service and dining to each guest, as well as booking signature spa treatments in one of the private pavilion suites.

130 Villen fügen sich in die herrliche Landschaft einer der größten Inseln im nördlichen Atoll von Malé ein. Zu jeder Gästevilla gehören ein privater, weißer Sandstrand oder ein privates Deck über dem kristallklaren, türkisblauen Wasser der Lagune. Etwa 20 Meter Abstand zwischen den in üppiger Vegetation eingebetteten Villen garantiert ungestörte Privatheit. In jeder Villa kümmert sich ein persönlicher Butler um Service und Speisen; er organisiert auch die Spa-Behandlungen in einer der privaten Pavillonsuiten.

130 villas s'intègrent dans le superbe paysage de l'une des plus grandes îles de l'atoll de Malé Nord. Chaque villa destinée aux visiteurs dispose de sa plage privée de sable blanc ou d'un deck privé au-dessus de l'eau bleu turquoise et transparente de la lagune. Le respect du domaine privé est garanti, les maisons associées à la végétation opulente étant toutes espacées de près de 20 mètres les unes des autres. Dans chaque villa, un serviteur s'occupe du service et des repas ; il organise également les soins du spa dans l'une des suites de pavillon privées.

130 villas salpican el cautivador paisaje de una de las islas mayores del atolón del Norte de Malé. Todas las villas cuenta con una playa privada de arena blanca o una terraza sobre el azul turquesa de la laguna. Los 20 metros de frondosa vegetación que separan unas villas de otras garantizan la máxima privacidad. Para cada una hay un mayordomo encargado del servicio y las comidas, que además organiza los tratamientos de spa ofrecidos en las suites privadas del pabellón.

130 ville si stagliano nel meraviglioso paesaggio di una delle più grandi isole dell'atollo settentrionale di Malé. Ad ogni villa appartiene una spiaggia privata di sabbia bianca o una terrazza sull'acqua azzurra e cristallina della laguna. Una distanza di circa 20 metri tra le case tuffate nella folta vegetazione garantisce assoluta privacy. In ogni villa, un devoto maggiordomo si occupa de servizio, dei pasti e dell'organizzazione dei trattamenti della spa in uno dei padiglioni privati.

Villas have high airy ceilings and generous exterior space, ranging from private verandas overlooking stretches of beach to private swimming pools with large decks.

Die Villen haben hohe, luftige Decken und großzügig bemessene Außenanlagen, von privaten Veranden mit Blick auf den Strand bis zu eigenen Swimmingpools mit großen Decks.

Les villas possèdent de hauts plafonds aérés et de vastes installations extérieures, des vérandas privées avec vue sur la plage aux piscines personnelles avec de grands decks.

Villas de techos elevados y aireados, en un recinto exterior perfectamente calculado de miradores privados y vistas a la playa y a la piscina privada con una amplia cubierta.

Le ville hanno soffitti alti e ariosi e spaziosi impianti esterni, dalle verande private con vista sulla spiaggia alle piscine dotate di vaste terrazze.

The interior design is Asian-island contemporary and elegantly tropical, using beautiful natural materials like bamboo arches, coconut shells, sea grass, and silks.

Die Innenräume sind zeitgenössisch im asiatischen Inselstil und tropischer Eleganz ausgestattet. Es dominieren schöne natürliche Materialien, wie Bambus, Kokosnussschalen, Seegras und Seide.

Les pièces intérieures sont dotées d'objets contemporains dans le style asiatique de l'île et de l'élégance tropicale. De beaux matériaux naturels sont mis en avant comme le bambou, les coques de noix de coco, la zostère et la soie.

Interiores contemporáneos al estilo asiático de la isla y dotados de la elegancia del trópico. En ellos dominan fabulosos materiales naturales, como el bambú, la cáscara de coco, la crin vegetal y la seda.

Gli interni, moderni, sono realizzati in stile isolano asiatico, con un tocco di eleganza tropicale. Prevalgono magnifici materiali naturali, come il bambù, i gusci di noce di cocco, le alghe e la seta.

Uma Paro

Paro, Bhutan

The country of the Thunder God in the Himalayas is hardly discovered by the tourist trade and the religious festivals, Buddhist temples and authenticity are enticing. Close to the cultural center of Paro, this luxurious retreat invites you to enjoy holistic regeneration. A stay in one of the nine villas with private spa promises recuperation with a spiritual note.

Das vom Tourismus noch kaum erschlossene Land des Donnergottes im Himalaya lockt mit religiösen Festen, buddhistischen Tempeln und durch seine Ursprünglichkeit. Nahe der Kulturhochburg Paro läd dieses luxuriöse Refugium zur ganzheitlichen Regeneration ein. Der Aufenthalt in einer der neun Villen mit privatem Spa verspricht Erholung mit spiritueller Note.

Très peu ouvert au tourisme, le pays du dieu du tonnerre dans l'Himalaya attire les visiteurs avec ses fêtes religieuses, ses temples bouddhistes et son originalité. À proximité du haut-lieu culturel de Paro, ce refuge luxurieux invite à une régénération totale. Lors de votre séjour dans l'une des neuf villas avec spa privé, vous bénéficierez de repos avec une note spirituelle.

En el Himalaya, un rincón apenas abierto al turismo en la tierra del Dios del trueno fascina con sus fiestas religiosas, templos budistas y su carácter primitivo. A poca distancia del centro cultural de Paro abre sus puertas un lujoso refugio destinado a regenerar en esencia. La estancia en una de las nueve villas con spa privado garantiza descanso con un toque espiritual.

Il Paese del dio del tuono nell'Himalaya, non ancora aperto al turismo, attira con le sue feste religiose, i templi buddisti e l'atmosfera dal sapore autentico. Nelle vicinanze di Paro, vera roccaforte di cultura, questo rifugio di lusso invita alla più completa rigenerazione. Il soggiorno in una delle nove ville con spa privata promette riposo e spiritualità.

Panoramic vistas overlooking the mountain landscape and meditative healing therapies enable the visitor from a western cultural hemisphere to indulge in a foreign world, influenced by the power of religion.

Panoramaausblicke in die Berglandschaft und meditative Wellness-therapien lassen den Besucher des westlichen Kulturkreises in eine fremde, von der Kraft der Religion geprägte Welt eintauchen.

Les vues panoramiques dans le paysage montagneux et les thérapies de wellness méditatives plongent le visiteur issu du milieu culturel occidental dans un monde étranger et imprégné de la force religieuse.

Las vistas panorámicas al paisaje montañoso y las terapias meditativas trasladan a los huéspedes de cultura occidental a un mundo aparte, invadido de fuerza religiosa.

Scorci panoramici sul paesaggio delle montagne e terapie wellness di tipo meditativo immergono il turista occidentale in un mondo lontano, pervaso dalla forza della religione.

Lavish carvings as well as traditional building style and healing methods reveal the influence of Buddhist culture.

Aufwändige Schnitzereien sowie traditioneller Baustil und Heilmethoden zeugen vom Einfluss der buddhistischen Kultur.

Les sculptures sur bois finement travaillées, ainsi que le style de construction traditionnel et les méthodes curatives, témoignent de l'influence de la culture bouddhiste.

Tallas exquisitas, estilo de construcción tradicional y métodos curativos dan testimonio de la influencia de la cultura budista.

I finissimi lavori d'intaglio, lo stile architettonico tradizionale ed i metodi terapeutici testimoniano l'influenza della cultura buddista.

The Plateau
Grand Hyatt Hong Kong
Hong Kong

This spa as a complete artwork, covering 80,000-square feet, shows how good architecture can also create a place of relaxation in the metropolitan jungle. Anybody leaving the elevator on the 11th floor of the Grand Hyatt steps onto the loosely-set stone parquet floor and acoustically—every step creates a sound—is already entering a fascinating roof-oasis with water follies, restaurant, sun decks and a 164-foot pool. All of this includes the best panoramic view and is rounded off with the fitness and treatment rooms as well as the signature 23 minimalist-design guest suites.

Dieses Spa-Gesamtkunstwerk auf 7400 Quadratmeter zeigt, wie gute Architektur auch im Großstadtdschungel einen Ort der Entspannung schaffen kann. Wer im 11. Stock des Grand Hyatt den Lift verlässt, tritt auf dem locker verlegten Steinparkett schon akustisch – jeder Schritt erzeugt einen Ton – in eine faszinierende Dachoase mit Wasserspielen, Restaurant, Sonnendecks und 50 Meter-Pool. Alles mit bester Panoramaaussicht und abgerundet mit den Fitness- und Behandlungsräumen sowie als Besonderheit, den 23 minimalistisch gestalteten Gäste-Suiten.

Ce spa, chef-d'oeuvre complet s'étendant sur 7400 mètres carrés, démontre que l'architecture de qualité peut également créer un lieu de détente dans la jungle des grandes villes. Lorsque le visiteur quitte l'ascenseur au 11ème étage du Grand Hyatt, il marche sur un parquet en pierres posé lâchement et pénètre déjà grâce à l'acoustique – chaque pas produit un son – dans un oasis fascinant aménagé sur le toit avec jeux d'eau, restaurant, ponts destinés au bain de soleil et piscine de 50 mètres. Le tout avec une superbe vue panoramique et complété par des pièces fitness et des pièces de soins ainsi qu'une particularité, 23 suites à l'aménagement minimaliste.

El spa, auténtica obra de arte en 7400 metros cuadrados, muestra cómo la buena arquitectura es capaz de crear un lugar para el descanso dentro del entramado de la gran ciudad. Salir del ascensor del piso 11 del Grand Hyatt y pisar el parquet de piedra suelta, que a cada paso produce un sonido diferente, implica ya sumergirse en un oasis fascinante, en un ático dotado de juegos de agua, restaurante, cubierta para tomar el sol y piscina de 50 metros. Todo ello frente a las mejores vistas panorámicas y completado con gimnasio, salas de tratamiento y 23 suites especiales de decoración minimalista.

Quest'opera d'arte totale con spa, che si estende su una superficie di 7400 metri quadrati, è la testimonianza di come la buona architettura possa realizzare un luogo di relax anche nella giungla cittadina. Chi lascia l'ascensore all'11 piano del Grand Hyatt e si avventura sul pavè entra anche acusticamente – al rumore di ogni passo – in un'affascinante oasi tra i tetti, fatta di giochi d'acqua, ristorante, terrazze, una piscina di 50 metri, circondata da una magnifica vista e dotata di sale per fitness e trattamenti, con 23 suite arredate in stile minimalista.

Drinking tea in a Zen roof garden or a wellness experience overlooking Hong Kong bay: connoisseurs will find fulfillment on the plateau.

Teetrinken in einem Zen-Dachgarten oder Wellness-Erlebnis mit Aussicht über die Bucht von Hongkong: im Plateau finden Ästheten ihre Erfüllung.

Boire le thé sur un toit en terrasse zen ou profiter d'un moment de wellness avec vue sur la baie de Hongkong : au Plateau, les esthètes trouveront satisfaction.

Tomar el té en un jardín Zen sobre la terraza o disfrutar del wellness con vistas a la bahía de Hong Kong: el Plateau es el sueño de los estetas.

Tè nell'attico zen o wellness con vista sulla baia di Hong Kong: il Plateau delizia il senso estetico dei suoi ospiti.

Architect John Edward Morford uses the minimalist design of the rooms to focus attention on eastern health doctrines.

Mit den minimalistisch gestalteten Räumen lenkt Architekt John Edward Morford die Aufmerksamkeit auf die östlichen Gesundheitslehren.

En mettant l'accent sur l'aménagement minimaliste des pièces, l'architecte John Edward Morford attire l'attention sur les principes d'hygiène orientaux.

El arquitecto John Edward Morford ha optado por una decoración minimalista de las habitaciones para desviar la atención hacia el estudio oriental sobre la salud.

Le sale in stile minimalista realizzate dall'architetto John Edward Morford concentrano l'attenzione sugli insegnamenti e sulle terapie orientali.

Sea-view sauna, multiple healing baths, beauty treatments, massages or fitness: the list of products incorporates many aspects.

Sauna mit Meerblick, vielerlei Heilbäder, Schönheitsbehandlungen, Massagen oder Fitness: die Angebotsliste umfasst viele Seiten.

Sauna avec vue sur la mer, multiples bains curatifs, soins de beauté, massages ou fitness : la liste des soins proposés est extrêmement variée.

Sauna con vistas al mar, los más diversos baños termales, tratamientos de belleza, masajes y gimnasio. La oferta no tiene límites.

Sauna con vista sul mare, bagni terapeutici di tutti i tipi, trattamenti estetici, massaggi o fitness: la lista delle possibilità è molto varia.

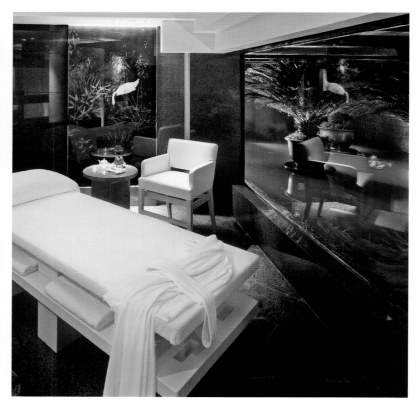

The Landmark
Mandarin Oriental Hong Kong

Hong Kong

A novelty in Hong Kong's hotel trade. The commission for designer duo Adam T. Tihany and Peter Remedios, working together here as a team for the first time, was a total endorsement for contemporary architecture by hotel group Mandarin Oriental. The minimum size of 16 square feet of the hotel's 113 rooms is real luxury in a metropolis, where space is in short supply. The themes of modern elegance and wellness are carried through the entire hotel from bathrooms to spa. The gourmet restaurant Amber on the 7th floor as well as the MO Bar have counted, since opening, among the city's most popular gastronomic addresses.

Eine Novität in Hongkongs Hotellerie. Mit der Beauftragung des Designerduos Adam T. Tihany und Peter Remedios, die hier erstmals im Team zusammenarbeiteten, setzte das Traditionsunternehmen Mandarin Oriental ganz auf zeitgenössische Architektur. Zu bewohnen ist sie in 113, mindestens 50 Quadratmeter großen Zimmern. Wahrer Luxus in einer Metropole, in der Platz Mangelware ist. Moderne Eleganz und Wellness sind die Themen, die sich durch das gesamte Haus ziehen, von den Badezimmern bis ins Spa. Das Gourmet-Restaurant Amber im 7. Stock sowie die MO Bar gehören seit ihrer Eröffnung zu den gefragtesten Gastronomie-Adressen in der Stadt.

Une nouveauté dans l'hôtellerie de Hongkong. En confiant l'agencement de l'hôtel au duo de designers Adam T. Tihany et Peter Remedios, qui ont travaillé ici pour la première fois en équipe, l'entreprise traditionnelle Mandarin Oriental a misé entièrement sur l'architecture contemporaine. Cet hôtel dispose de 113 chambres d'une surface minimum de 50 mètres carrés : un véritable luxe dans une métropole où la place constitue une denrée rare. L'élégance moderne et le wellness sont des themes récurrents dans tout l'ensemble, des salles de bain au spa. Le restaurant pour gourmets Amber installé au 7ème étage ainsi que le MO Bar comptent depuis leur ouverture parmi les adresses gastronomiques les plus demandées de la ville.

Una novedad en la hostelería de Hong Kong. Al ofrecer el proyecto a la pareja de diseñadores Adam T. Tihany y Peter Remedios, en su primer trabajo en común, la casa de tradición del Mandarin Oriental apostó por una arquitectura absolutamente contemporánea. El edificio dispone de 113 habitaciones, las más pequeñas de 50 metros cuadrados. Todo un lujo en una ciudad que sufre la carencia de espacio. Elegancia moderna y wellness son los temas presentes en toda la casa, desde los baños hasta el spa. En el piso 7, el restaurante para gourmets Amber y el MO Bar se han convertido en dos de las direcciones gastronómicas más solicitadas de la ciudad.

Una novità tra gli hotel di Hong Kong. Incaricando del progetto i designer Adam T. Tihany e Peter Remedios, che hanno lavorato insieme per la prima volta, la tradizionale impresa Mandarin Oriental ha puntato su uno stile architettonico assolutamente contemporaneo, fatto di 113 camere, delle dimensioni minime di 50 metri quadrati. Un vero lusso in una metropoli in cui lo spazio è una merce rara. Moderna eleganza e wellness sono i temi che si snodano in tutto il complesso, dai bagni alla spa. Il ristorante per gourmet Amber al 7 piano ed il MO Bar sono stati, sin dalla loro apertura, tra gli indirizzi gastronomici più richiesti della città.

The hotel is connected to a new commercial and shopping center by a network of canopied pedestrian bridges.

Durch ein Netz aus überdachten Fußgängerbrücken ist das Hotel mit einem neuen Geschäfts- und Einkaufszentrum verbunden.

L'hôtel est relié au nouveau centre d'affaires et commercial par un réseau de ponts couverts pour piétons.

El hotel comunica con un centro comercial nuevo a través de una red de puentes cubiertos para peatones.

L'hotel è collegato al nuovo centro commerciale da una rete di ponti pedonali coperti.

Amethyst crystal steam baths, revitalizing swimming pools, adventure showers as well as Asia's first rasul bath are included in treatments offered by The Oriental Spa located on two floors.

Zu den Angeboten des The Oriental Spa, das sich über zwei Stockwerke erstreckt, gehören Amethyst-Kristall-Dampfbäder, vitalisierende Swimmingpools, Erlebnis-Duschen sowie Asiens erstes Rasulbad.

Installé sur deux étages, The Oriental Spa propose entre autres des bains de vapeur d'améthyste et de cristal, des piscines revigorantes, des douches originales ainsi que le premier bain Rasul d'Asie.

Entre las propuestas del The Oriental Spa de dos plantas, figuran baños de cristal y amatista, piscinas revitalizantes, duchas de relax, sin olvidar el primer baño Rasul de Asia.

Tra le attrazioni della The Oriental Spa, situata su due piani, fanno parte i bagni turchi ai cristalli d'ametista, le piscine rivitalizzanti, le docce emozionali ed il primo bagno Rasul di tutta l'Asia.

The Lalu

Sun Moon Lake, Taiwan

It used to be the Japanese Imperial family's summer palace, later, the first Taiwanese president lived here. The view over Sun Moon Lake is regal, the building, which Kerry Hill refined into an architectural masterpiece in 1998, is presidential. Earthy colors coincide with straight lines; wood on stone and glass. The building's interior, the landscape design and unspoiled nature create a sense of unity. In this environment, which is already soothing, the spa offers extra pampering with a combination of western and eastern treatments.

Einst war es der Sommerpalast der japanischen Kaiserfamilie, später bewohnte es der erste taiwanesische Präsident. Königlich gibt sich die Aussicht über den Sun Moon Lake, präsidial das Gebäude, das Kerry Hill 1998 zu einem architektonischen Meisterstück veredelt hat. Erdige Farben treffen auf gerade Linien, Holz auf Stein und Glas. Gebäudeinneres, Landschaftsgestaltung und urwüchsige Natur bilden eine Einheit. In dieser schon an sich wohltuenenden Umgebung verwöhnt das Spa zusätzlich mit einer Kombination aus westlichen und östlichen Behandlungen.

Il s'agissait autrefois du palais d'été de la famille impériale japonaise. Le premier président taiwanais y résida plus tard. La vue sur le Sun Moon Lake est royale, le bâtiment, transformé en 1998 par Kerry Hill en chef-d'œuvre architectural, est quant à lui présidentiel. Les couleurs de terre rencontrent des lignes droites, le bois rencontre la pierre et le verre. L'intérieur du bâtiment, l'agencement du paysage et la nature à l'état sauvage créent une unité. Dans cet environnement déjà bénéfique, le spa offre une sensation bienfaisante supplémentaire avec une combinaison de soins occidentaux et orientaux.

Lo que en su día fue el palacio de verano de la familia imperial japonesa, estuvo habitado posteriormente por el presidente de Taiwán. Una vista majestuosa al Sun Moon Lake, preside el edificio que en 1998 Kerry Hill coronó como obra de arte arquitectónica. Los tonos ocre se difuminan entre líneas rectas, la madera se funde con la piedra y el cristal. Los interiores, la concepción del paisaje y la naturaleza salvaje forman un todo. En este entorno grato de por sí el spa agasaja con una combinación de tratamientos orientales y occidentales.

Una volta era la residenza estiva della famiglia imperiale giapponese, in seguito divenne la dimora del primo presidente taiwanese. Nel 1998 Kerry Hill ha trasformato in un capolavoro d'architettura questo edificio dall'aspetto presidenziale, impreziosito da una magnifica vista sul lago Sun Moon. I colori della terra s'incontrano con linee diritte, il legno si sposa con la pietra e il vetro. Gli interni, il paesaggio e la natura selvaggia costituiscono un unico insieme. In quest'atmosfera già di per sé così benefica, la spa vizia gli ospiti con una combinazione di trattamenti occidentali ed orientali.

The minimalist and open architecture support the location's meditative atmosphere.

Die minimalistische und offene Architektur unterstützen die meditative Atmosphäre des Ortes.

L'architecture minimaliste et ouverte souligne l'atmosphère méditative du lieu.

La abierta arquitectura minimalista reafirma la atmósfera de meditación del lugar.

L'architettura minimalista, con i suoi ampi spazi, pone l'accento sul carattere meditativo del luogo.

From the spa and all 96 suites, the neighboring mountains and jade-green Sun Moon Lake—Taiwan's largest freshwater lake—are visible.

Vom Spa und jeder der 96 Suiten aus sind die angrenzenden Berge und der jadegrüne Sun Moon Lake, Taiwans größter Süßwassersee, zu sehen.

Le spa et les 96 suites permettent d'admirer les montagnes voisines et le Sun Moon Lake vert jade, le plus grand lac d'eau douce de Taiwan.

Desde el spa y cada una de las 96 suites las vistas abarcan las montañas cercanas y el verde jade del mayor lago de agua dulce de Taiwán, el Sun Moon Lake.

Dalla spa e da ognuna delle 96 suite si possono ammirare le vicine montagne ed il più grande lago d'acqua dolce di Taiwan, Sun Moon, dal verde intenso di giada.

Park Hyatt Seoul

Seoul, South Korea

Set directly in the trade center in the commercial district of Gangnam, the hotel's 24 floors are surprising, due to their generosity and modernity, which you would not expect in the heart of an international city. The Japanese designer team Super Potato created all 185 rooms in the style of private mini-lofts, with dark wooden floors, room dividers and plenty of transparency. The bathrooms with raw natural stone walls are partitioned by glass walls, the 11 foot floor-to-ceiling windows overlook Seoul's skyline, which is only surpassed by the view from the lobby on the top floor.

Direkt am Messezentrum im Geschäftsviertel Gangnam gelegen, überrascht das 24 Stockwerke umfassende Hotel mit einer Modernität und Großzügigkeit, die man nicht im Zentrum einer Weltstadt erwarten würde. Die japanische Designergruppe Super Potato gestaltete die 185 Zimmer im Stil privater Mini-Lofts, mit dunklen Holzdielenböden, Raumteilern und viel Transparenz. Die Badezimmer mit rohen Natursteinwänden sind mit Glaswänden abgetrennt, die vom Boden bis zur Decke reichenden 3,40 Meter hohen Fenster bieten eine Aussicht auf Seouls Skyline, die nur noch von der aus der Lobby in der obersten Etage übertroffen wird.

Situé tout près du centre des expositions dans le quartier des affaires de Gangnam, l'hôtel de 24 étages surprend avec une modernité et une générosité à laquelle on ne s'attendrait pas dans le centre d'une grande ville de renommée mondiale. Le groupe de designers japonais Super Potato a aménagé les 185 pièces dans le style de mini-lofts privés, avec des planchers en bois sombre, des séparations de pièces et beaucoup de transparence. Les salles de bain, dont les murs sont en pierre naturelle brut, sont séparées par des murs de verre. Les fenêtres de 3,40 mètres de haut, allant du sol au plafond, offrent une vue imprenable sur la skyline de Séoul que seule la vue obtenue dans le lobby situé au dernier étage surpasse.

Junto al recinto ferial del barrio de negocios Gangnam, se levanta este hotel de 24 plantas sorprendiendo con una modernidad y generosidad que no se espera encontrar en el centro de una gran ciudad. El equipo de diseño Super Potato concibió las 185 habitaciones a modo de mini lofts privados, con suelos de tarima oscura, separadores de ambientes y un derroche de transparencia. Los cuartos de baño están revestidos de paredes desnudas de piedra y separados por cristaleras. Los ventanales de suelo a techo de 3,40 metros ofrecen unas espectaculares vistas al horizonte de Seúl, que tan sólo comparte el vestíbulo de la última planta.

Situato nel quartiere commerciale di Gangnam, nelle dirette vicinanze del centro fieristico, questo hotel di 24 piani sorprende per la sua modernità e spaziosità , che il turista non si aspetterebbe nel centro di una metropoli. Il gruppo di designer giapponesi Super Potato ha realizzato le 185 camere nello stile di tante miniloft private, luminosissime, con pavimenti di legno scuro e mobili divisori. I bagni, dai muri in pietra, hanno pareti divisorie in vetro, mentre le finestre, che si allungano dal pavimento al soffitto e sono alte 3,40 metri, si affacciano sullo skyline di Seoul: una vista superata soltanto da quella che si gode dalla lobby all'ultimo piano.

Despite, or rather because it is a business hotel, the Hyatt promotes wellness in all rooms as well as in the Park Club Spa, with heated indoor pool, or in the fitness center with a view.

Obwohl oder gerade weil es sich um ein Geschäftshotel handelt, setzt Hyatt durchweg auf Wellness, in den Zimmern sowie im Park Club Spa mit beheiztem Hallenbad oder im Fitnesszentrum mit Aussicht.

Bien qu'il s'agisse d'un hôtel d'affaires, ou plus précisément pour cette raison, Hyatt mise sans exception sur le wellness, dans les chambres tout comme dans le Park Club Spa avec piscine couverte chauffée ou dans le centre de fitness avec panorama.

Aunque se trate de un hotel de negocios, o quizá precisamente por eso, el Hyatt apuesta por el wellness, ya sea en las habitaciones, en el Park Club Spa con piscina climatizada o en el gimnasio.

Sebbene si tratti di un hotel business – o forse proprio per questo motivo – Hyatt punta completamente sul wellness, sia nelle camere sia nella Park Club spa con piscina riscaldata, sia nel centro fitness con vista panoramica.

1,200-square foot is the size of the Diplomatic Suite, but measuring 560-square feet the "normal" rooms are still as large as an average city apartment.

112 Quadratmeter misst die Diplomatic-Suite, die normalen Zimmer haben mit 52 Quadratmeter aber immer noch die Größe eines durchschnittlichen Stadt-Appartements.

La suite Diplomatic compte 112 mètres carrés, mais les chambres « normales » d'une surface de 52 mètres carrés disposent encore de la taille d'un appartement de ville moyen.

La suite diplomatica è grande 112 metri quadrati, mentre le camere "normali" raggiungono, con i loro 52 metri quadrati, le dimensioni medie di un monolocale cittadino.

La Diplomatic Suite abarca 112 metros cuadrados, mientras que las "normales" cuentan con 52 metros cuadrados, que no dejan de ser las dimensiones de media de un apartamento en la ciudad.

Grand Hyatt Erawan Bangkok

Bangkok, Thailand

One of the main attractions of this 380-room business hotel on the centrally located Rajdamri Road is the new i.sawan Residential Spa & Club. A 75,000-square foot wellness facility in parkland with 82-foot pool, tennis court, sauna-steam bath, fitness center, the Breezeway restaurant, nine treatment as well as six guest bungalows, perfect for relaxation. In contrast to the traditional hotel building, this Tony Chi-designed facility is minimalist. The pictures might suggest a park location, but the secret is that it is located on the roof of the fifth floor.

Eine der Hauptattraktionen dieses 380-Zimmer-Geschäftshotels an der zentral gelegenen Rajdamri Road ist der neue i.sawan Residential Spa & Club. Eine 7000 Quadratmeter große Wellness-Einrichtung im Grünen, mit 25-Meter-Pool, Tennisplatz, Sauna-Dampfbad, Fitnesszentrum, dem Restaurant Breezeway, neun Behandlungs- sowie sechs zur Erholung optimierten Gästebungalows. Im Gegensatz zum traditionellen Hotelgebäude ist die von Designer Tony Chi gestaltete Anlage minimalistisch. Der Clou, sie befindet sich nicht, wie aus den Bildern zu vermuten wäre, in einem Park, sondern auf dem Dach des fünften Stockwerks.

L'une des attractions principales de cet hôtel d'affaires de 380 chambres situé sur la Rajdamri Road centrale est le nouveau i.sawan Residential Spa & Club. Une installation wellness de 7000 mètres carrés en pleine nature, avec piscine de 25 mètres, terrain de tennis, bain de vapeur avec sauna, centre de fitness, le restaurant Breezeway, neuf bungalows destinés aux soins ainsi que six bungalows de visiteurs optimisés pour le repos. Contrairement au bâtiment de l'hôtel traditionnel, le complexe aménagé par le designer Tony Chi est minimaliste. Le clou ne se trouve pas, comme on pourrait le supposer à partir des images, dans le parc, mais sur le toit du cinquième étage.

El i.sawan Residential Spa & Club es sin duda una de las principales atracciones de este hotel de negocios de 380 habitaciones, con ubicación central en la Rajdamri Road. Las instalaciones del wellness abarcan 7000 metros cuadrados de zona verde, con piscina de 25 metros, pista de tenis, baño de vapor, sauna, gimnasio, el restaurante Breezeway, nueve bungalows para tratamientos y seis concebidos para el relax de los huéspedes. Al contrario que los edificios de hotel tradicionales, la construcción del diseñador Tony Chi es plenamente minimalista. La mayor atracción no se encuentra en el parque, como pueda parecer en las fotos sino en el tejado del quinto piso.

Una delle principali attrazioni di questo hotel business di 380 camere situato nella centralissima Rajdamri Road, è il nuovo i.sawan Residential Spa & Club, un edificio per il wellness che si estende su una superficie di 7000 metri quadrati, in mezzo al verde, con una piscina di 25 metri, campo da tennis, sauna, bagno turco, centro fitness, il ristorante Breezeway, nove bungalow per i trattamenti e sei destinati al relax. In contrasto con l'edificio, di stampo tradizionale, il complesso, realizzato dal designer Tony Chi, è in stile minimalista. La sorpresa: esso non si trova in un parco, come lasciano presumere le foto, bensì sul tetto del quinto piano.

Surrounded by the hectic bustle of the Asian major city, the i.sawan spa as well as the garden with pool reveal an enclave of tranquility. At the poolside, a teakwood deck or one of the 56 sun-loungers invite guests to relax.

Umgeben vom hektischen Treiben der asiatischen Großstadt präsentiert sich das i.sawan Spa sowie der Garten mit Pool als Enklave der Ruhe. Am Poolrand laden ein Teakholzdeck oder eine der 56 Sonnenlounges zur Entspannung ein.

Entouré par l'agitation hectique de la grande ville asiatique, le spa i.sawan, tout comme le jardin avec piscine, se présentent comme une enclavede calme. Au bord de la piscine, le pont en teck ou l'un des 56 salons destinés au bain de soleil invitent à la détente.

Envuelto en el ajetreo de la enorme ciudad asiática, el i.sawan spa y el jardín con piscina son un verdadero remanso de serenidad. La cubiertade teca y las 56 tumbonas para tomar el sol entorno a la piscina invitan al relax.

Circondati dalla vita frenetica della metropoli asiatica, sia l'i.sawan spa sia il giardino con piscina, si presentano come un'oasi di tranquillità. Ai bordi della piscina, la terrazza in teak o uno dei 56 solarium invitano al relax.

Next to the spacious bath, the Residential Spa Cottages have bedrooms, residential and treatment rooms as well as a private terrace.

Neben dem geräumigen Bad verfügen die Residential Spa Cottages über Schlaf-, Wohn- und Behandlungszimmer sowie über eine eigene Terrasse.

Parallèlement à la salle de bain spacieuse, les Residential Spa Cottages disposent d'une chambre à coucher, d'un salon et d'une pièce destinée aux soins ainsi que de leur propre terrasse.

Además de un amplio baño, las Residential Spa Cottages están dotadas de dormitorio, sala de estar, sala para tratamientos y terraza propia.

Oltre allo spazioso bagno, i Residential Spa Cottages dispongono di camera da letto, soggiorno, saletta per il trattamento e terrazza privata.

Mandarin Oriental Dhara Dhevi

Chiang Mai, Thailand

65 villas, 58 suites and two themed residential facilities are created as a luxurious tourist village on the perimeter of the north-Thai cultural resort of Chiang Mai. The resort's building style follows traditional Lanna architecture, which is famous for its pitched roofs, decorated with carvings. For physical well being, The Dhevi Spa offers a menu, which inspires guests to meditative regeneration. With its 25 treatment rooms, the site is built in the style of the Mandalay Palace in Myanmar and consciously radiates a fairytale atmosphere.

65 Villen, 58 Suiten und zwei Themen-Residenzen formen sich am Rande der nordthailändischen Kulturdestination Chiang Mai zu einem luxuriösen Gästedorf. In ihrem Baustil folgt das Resort der traditionellen Lanna-Architektur, die für ihre mit Schnitzereien versehenen Spitzdächer bekannt ist. Für das körperliche Wohlbefinden bietet The Dhevi Spa ein Menü, das Gäste zur meditativen Regeneration anregt. Die Anlage mit ihren 25 Behandlungsräumen ist dem Mandalay Palast in Myanmar nachempfunden und strahlt eine ganz bewusst märchenhafte Atmosphäre aus.

65 villas, 58 suites et deux résidences à thème sont réunies au bord de la destination culturelle Chiang Mai du Nord de la Thaïlande pour former un village de luxe pour les visiteurs. Le style de construction du complexe s'inspire de l'architecture traditionnelle Lanna, connue pour ses toits pointus pourvus de sculptures sur bois. Pour le bien-être corporel, The Dhevi Spa propose un menu qui incite les visiteurs à la régénération méditative. Avec 25 pièces destinées aux soins, le complexe ressemble au Palais Mandalay de Myanmar et dégage volontairement une atmosphère fantastique.

65 villas, 58 suites y dos residencias temáticas se reúnen formando una población de lujo entorno a uno de los destinos culturales al Norte de Tailandia, Chiang Mai. El estilo de construcción, famoso por sus tejados tallados apuntados, se mantiene fiel a la tradicional arquitectura Lanna. Del bienestar corporal se encarga el The Dhevi Spa, con un menú destinado a la regeneración meditativa de sus huéspedes. El establecimiento, que cuenta con 25 salas de tratamiento, está construido a imagen del palacio Mandalay de Myanmar y desprende intencionadamente un ambiente de fábula.

65 ville, 58 suite e due residenze a tema formano un lussuoso villaggio turistico ai margini di Chiang Mai, località della Tailandia settentrionale nota per il patrimonio culturale. Lo stile del resort si ispira all'architettura tradizionale Lanna, nota per i tetti a punta ricchi di intarsi. Per il benessere fisico, The Dhevi Spa offre un menu che stimola la rigenerazione meditativa. Il complesso, con 25 sale per i trattamenti, è costruito su imitazione del palazzo Mandalay di Myanmar ed irradia un'autentica atmosfera da fiaba.

Between rice fields and tropical vegetation, wooden walkways are installed to connect residential buildings with spa, lobby, library as well as six restaurants and cafés.

Zwischen Reisfeldern und tropischer Vegetation eingesetzte Holzstege verbinden die Wohngebäude mit Spa, Lobby, Bibliothek sowie sechs Restaurants und Cafés.

Les passerelles en bois installées entre les rizières et la végétation tropicale relient les bâtiments d'habitation au spa, au lobby, à la bibliothèque ainsi qu'aux six restaurants et cafés.

Entre campos de arroz y vegetación tropical senderos de madera enlazan los edificios de vivienda con el spa, vestíbulo, biblioteca y los seis restaurantes y cafés.

Tra le risaie e la vegetazione tropicale, passerelle di legno collegano gli edifici residenziali con la spa, la lobby, la biblioteca e con sei ristoranti e caffè.

Light, mostly creamy color tones as well as interiors in colonial style create a contrast to the Lanna architecture of the building's shell.

Helle, meist cremige Farbtöne sowie Interieur im Kolonialstil erzeugen einen Kontrast zur Lanna-Architektur der Gebäudehülle.

Les tons clairs et la plupart du temps crèmes, ainsi que l'intérieur réalisé dans un style colonial, créent un contraste par rapport à l'architecture Lanna de l'enveloppe du bâtiment.

Tonos claros, predominantemente color crema, e interiores de estilo colonial crean contraste con la arquitectura Lanna de la estructura del edificio.

Tonalità chiare, per lo più color crema, ed interni in stile coloniale fanno da contrasto all'architettura Lanna degli esterni.

Most suites also partially have a canopied wooden terrace. Some even have a private revitalizing pool.

Die meisten Suiten haben eine teilweise auch überdachte Holzterrasse. Einige besitzen sogar ihren eigenen Erfrischungspool.

La plupart des suites disposent d'une terrasse en bois partiellement couverte. Certaines possèdent même leur propre piscine de rafraîchissement.

La mayor parte de las suites cuentan con una terraza de madera semicubierta. Algunas incluso disfrutan de una mini piscina.

La maggior parte delle suite dispone di una terrazza di legno parzialmente coperta. Alcune sono fornite anche di piscina rinfrescante privata.

Evason Hideaway & Six Senses Spa at Hua Hin

Hua Hin, Thailand

If luxury primarily means space, then the setting of the Hideaway on the Gulf of Thailand, south of the royal city of Hua Hin, counts amongst the absolute highlights. The smallest of the 55 guest villas measures 2,669-square feet, the pool-villa suites with two bedrooms extend to 4,407-square feet. The earth spa is also unique, with its clay huts being built in the style of north-Thai villages. They house four treatment rooms and a meditation cave, whose openings ensure natural air circulation and a pleasant cooling effect.

Wenn Luxus vor allem auch Raum bedeutet, dann gehört das am Golf von Thailand, südlich der Königstadt Hua Hin gelegene Hideaway zu den absoluten Highlights. Die kleinsten der 55 Gästevillen messen 248 Quadratmeter, die Poolvilla-Suiten mit zwei Schlafräumen bringen es auf 376 Quadratmeter. Einzigartig ist auch der Earthspa, dessen Lehmhäuser nach dem Vorbild von Dörfern im Norden Thailands gebaut wurden. Sie beherbergen vier Behandlungsräume und eine Meditationshöhle, deren Öffnungen für natürliche Luftzirkulation und angenehme Kühle sorgen.

L'espace étant ici avant tout synonyme de luxe, cette retraite située dans le Golfe de Thaïlande au sud de la ville royale de Hua Hin compte parmi les highlights absolus. Parmi les 55 villas de visiteurs, les plus petites disposent d'une surface de 248 mètres carrés, celle des suites villa et piscine avec deux chambres à coucher atteint 376 mètres carrés. Le domaine Earthspa est également unique, ses maisons en argile ont été construites d'après le modèle de villages dans le Nord de la Thaïlande. Elles hébergent quatre pièces destinées aux soins et une grotte de méditation présentant des ouvertures afin de garantir la circulation naturelle de l'air et une fraîcheur agréable.

Si por lujo se entiende sobretodo espacio entonces este refugio ubicado en el Golfo de Tailandia, al sur de la ciudad imperial de Hua Hin es el más absoluto triunfador. De las 55 villas, las más pequeñas miden 248 metros cuadrados, mientras que las suites con piscina y dos dormitorios cuentan con 376 metros cuadrados. Inigualable lo es también el Earthspa, construcción de casas de adobe al estilo de los pueblos del norte del país, que alberga cuatro salas para tratamientos y una cueva para meditación, con ranuras de circulación de aire natural para proporcionar frescor.

Se lusso significa in primo luogo spazio, anche questo hideaway, situato sul Golfo di Tailandia, a sud della città reale di Hua Hin, fa parte dei luoghi di prim'ordine. Le più piccole tra le 55 ville hanno una superficie di 248 metri quadri, mentre le suite delle ville con piscina, dotate di due camere da letto, raggiungono i 376 metri quadrati. Unica è anche la Earthspa, le cui case d'argilla sono state costruite come quelle dei villaggi della Tailandia settentrionale: esse ospitano quattro cabine per i trattamenti ed una grotta per la meditazione, le cui aperture permettono all'aria di circolare naturalmente e di mantenere una temperatura piacevolmente fresca.

A secluded setting, in tropical vegetation, directly behind the extended sandy beach of Pranburi. This is the luxurious sister to the neighboring and far larger Evason Hua Hin Resort.

Abgeschottet, in tropischer Vegetation, gleich hinter dem kilometerlangen Sandstrand von Pranburi liegt dieser luxuriöse Ableger des benachbarten und weitaus größeren Evason Hua Hin Resort.

Cette filiale luxurieuse du complexe voisin Evason Hua Hin, largement plus grand, est isolée dans la végétation tropicale, juste derrière la plage de sable de Pranburi qui s'étend sur plusieurs kilomètres.

Esta prolongación del vasto Evason Hua Hin Resort se esconde entre la vegetación tropical, justo detrás de la quilométrica playa de Pranburi.

Questa lussuosa dépendance del vicino e molto più grande resort Evason Hua Hin è situata tra la vegetazione tropicale, subito dietro la lunghissima spiaggia sabbiosa di Pranburi.

Designed as an exclusive villa resort, the Hideaway, promotes pure regeneration and privacy. Anyone who still prefers to leave his sanctuary will find Mediterranean food in the beach restaurant.

Das als exklusive Villenanlage konzipierte Hideaway setzt ganz auf Wellness und Privatsphäre. Wer sein Refugium dennoch verlassen möchte, findet im Strandrestaurant mediterrane Kost.

Cette retraite, conçue sous la forme d'un complexe exclusif de villas, mise entièrement sur le wellness et le caractère privé. Ceux qui souhaitent toutefois quitter leur refuge pourront déguster de la cuisine méditerranéenne au restaurant de la plage.

El exclusivo complejo de villas escondite apuesta por el bienestar y la privacidad, sin privar a quienes deseen abandonar este refugio y disfrutar de la cocina mediterránea en un restaurante de playa.

Concepito come un esclusivo complesso di ville, l'Hideaway punta completamente su wellness ed intimità. Chi, tuttavia, desidera uscire dal suo rifugio, può gustare le specialità mediterranee del ristorante sulla spiaggia.

Sila Evason Hideaway & Spa at Samui

Koh Samui, Thailand

On a promontory at the northern end of Thailand's second largest island, Koh Samui, the hotel chain Six Senses known for its minimalist-romantic architecture, has created a sanctuary that truly appeals to all the senses. Untreated wood, bamboo poles, unhewn stone, handcrafted lights and furniture coincide with giant grassy areas and straight-lined pools that melt seamlessly into the horizon. Here, purism and luxury form a rare harmonious unity, which further emphasizes the Hideaway Spa, built into the cliffs.

Auf einer Landzunge am nördlichen Ende von Thailands zweitgrößter Insel Koh Samui hat die für ihre minimalistisch-romantische Architektur bekannte Hotelgruppe Six Senses ein Refugium errichtet, das in der Tat alle Sinne anzusprechen vermag. Rohes Holz, Bambusstangen, unbehauener Stein, kunsthandwerkliche Leuchten und Möbel treffen auf riesige Glasflächen und geradlinige Pools, die randlos mit dem Horizont verschmelzen. Purismus und Luxus bilden hier eine selten harmonische Einheit, die das in die Klippen gebaute Hideaway Spa noch unterstreicht.

C'est sur une langue de terre à l'extrémité nord de la deuxième île la plus grande de Thaïlande, Koh Samui, que le groupe hôtelier Six Senses, connu pour son architecture minimaliste et romantique, a créé un refuge faisant réellement appel à tous les sens. Bois brut, barres de bambou, pierre non taillée, lustres et meubles artisanaux sont associés à de géantes surfaces en verre et à des piscines aux contours droits qui se fondent sans rebord dans l'horizon. Le purisme et le luxe créent ici une rare unité harmonieuse qui souligne encore le Hideaway Spa construit dans les rochers.

En una lengua de tierra de la segunda mayor isla de Koh Samui, al extremo norte de Tailandia, el grupo hotelero Six Senses, conocido por su estilo romántico y minimalista ha creado un refugio de placer destinado a estimular los sentidos. Madera desbastada, bambú, piedra sin labrar, iluminación y muebles artesanales en comunión con enormes estructuras de cristal y piscinas de líneas rectas, que se funden en el horizonte. Purismo y lujo forman una inusual unidad armónica, acentuada aún si cabe con el Hideaway Spa construido en un acantilado.

Su una lingua di terra nella parte settentrionale della seconda isola più grande della Tailandia, Koh Samui, il gruppo alberghiero Six Senses, noto per l'architettura di gusto romantico-minimalista, ha costruito un rifugio in grado di deliziare veramente tutti i sensi. Legno e pietra grezzi, bambù, lumi e mobili artigianali incontrano sconfinate superfici di vetro e piscine lineari, i cui bordi si fondono con l'orizzonte. Purismo e lusso formano qui un'unità armonica rara, a cui l'Hideaway Spa, costruita tra gli scogli, dà il tocco finale.

Untreated wooden panels or simple fittings illustrate the Six Senses philosophy, for which true luxury means simplicity.

Rohe Holzpaneele oder schlichte Armaturen veranschaulichen die Philosophie von Six Senses, für die sich wahrer Luxus archetypisch gibt.

Les panneaux de bois brut et les armatures simples illustrent la philosophie de Six Senses qui défend le caractère archétype du véritable luxe.

Paneles de madera desbastada y accesorios austeros como espejo de la filosofía del Six Senses, arquetipo del lujo.

Pannelli di legno grezzo e rubinetterie lineari esprimono la filosofia di Six Senses, per il quale il vero lusso è un archetipo.

Bamboo poles are repeatedly used here: in one case as a bathroom wall, elsewhere, they are used for garden or landscape architecture, as here, for light-installations around the swimming pool.

Bambusstangen kommen hier vielfältig zum Einsatz: einmal als Badezimmerwand, an anderer Stelle dienen sie der Garten- und Landschaftsarchitektur, wie hier für die Lichtobjekte um das Schwimmbad.

Les barres de bambou sont utilisées de différentes façons : comme paroi de salle de bain, mais elles servent également d'élément architectural dans le jardin et dans le paysage, comme ici pour les objets lumineux autour de la piscine.

Las varas de bambú aparecen con los más diversos usos, ya sea como pared del baño, para la arquitectura paisajística y de jardín o bien para los objetos de iluminación entorno a la piscina.

Il bambù viene utilizzato in mille modi: come parete in bagno, come elemento architettonico nei giardini, o per illuminare la piscina.

The undulating landscape surrounding the resort plays a central role together with the sea. The buildings are correspondingly open and transparent.

Die das Resort umgebene Hügellandschaft und das Meer spielen die Hauptrolle. Entsprechend offen und transparent sind die Gebäude.

Le paysage de collines et la mer qui entourent le complexe jouent le rôle principal. Les bâtiments sont par conséquent ouverts et transparents.

La atención se centra en el mar y el paisaje de colinas que rodea al resort. Para ello los edificios son abiertos y transparentes.

Il paesaggio collinare circostante e il mare sono i veri protagonisti: anche gli edifici sono ampi e luminosi.

Sala Samui Resort and Spa

Koh Samui, Thailand

Set on the previously almost untouched Choeng Mon Beach in the northeast of the island, this boutique resort with 69 luxury villas creates a unique style of traditional architecture and contemporary ambiance. White walls, cushions, linen covers and fabric tracks compliment each other, together with the selectively utilized dark wood on the walls, flooring and furniture items. Many people dream of an interior like this for a holiday home. Here, you can try living in your dream, inclusive of private pool and Mandara spa.

Am bisher noch kaum berührten Choeng-Mon-Strand im Nordosten der Insel prägt dieses Boutique-Resort mit 69 Luxusvillen einen eigenen Stil aus traditioneller Architektur und zeitgenössischem Ambiente. Weiße Wände, Polster, Leinenbezüge und Stoffbahnen ergänzen sich mit den behutsam eingesetzten dunklen Hölzern an Wänden, Böden und Möbelstücken. Eine Einrichtung, wie sie sich viele für ein Ferienhaus erträumen. Hier kann man den Traum Probe wohnen, inklusive privatem Pool und Mandara-Spa.

Au Nord-Est de l'île, le long de la plage de Choeng Mon encore quasiment intacte jusqu'ici, cet hôtel-boutique présente son propre style d'architecture traditionnelle et d'ambiance contemporaine avec 69 villas de luxe. Murs blancs, rembourrage, revêtements en lin et bandes de tissu sont complétés par le bois sombre soigneusement apposé aux murs, aux sols et aux meubles. Nombreuses sont les personnes qui rêveraient d'une telle installation pour leur maison de vacances. Elles peuvent ici obtenir un échantillon de leur rêve, piscine privée et spa Mandara inclus.

En la apenas explotada playa de Choeng Mon, al norte de la isla se ubica un Boutique-Resort con 69 villas de lujo y un estilo propio que intercala arquitectura tradicional y ambiente contemporáneo. Paredes blancas, tapicería, fundas de lino y tiras de tela se complementan con las maderas oscuras cuidadosamente integradas en las paredes, suelos y mobiliario. La decoración ideal para una casa de vacaciones; un sueño que se puede probar con piscina y spa Mandara incluidos.

Sulla spiaggia di Choeng Mon, nella parte nordorientale dell'isola, ancora intatta, questo boutique resort con 69 lussuose ville si distingue per il caratteristico stile fatto di architettura tradizionale e di atmosfera contemporanea: pareti bianche, mobili imbottiti, fodere di lino e passerelle di stoffa si integrano magnificamente con il legno scuro – utilizzato con la dovuta parsimonia – delle pareti, dei pavimenti e dei mobili. Un arredamento che molti sognerebbero per una residenza di villeggiatura. Ma qui è possibile vivere il sogno, con incluse la piscina privata e la Mandara Spa.

Choose from villas with one or two bedrooms. All of them have a spacious, semi-open bath and terrace. 53 have their own mini-swimming pool.

Zur Auswahl stehen Villen mit einem oder zwei Schlafzimmern. Alle verfügen sie über ein geräumiges, halboffenes Bad und Terrasse. 53 von ihnen haben ihr eigenes Mini-Schwimmbad.

Au choix, des villas comprenant une ou deux chambres à coucher. Toutes disposent d'une salle de bain spacieuse semi-ouverte et d'une terrasse. Parmi elles, 53 possèdent leur propre mini-piscine.

La elección está entre villas con una o con dos habitaciones. Todas cuentan con un amplio baño semiabierto además de terraza y 53 de ellas disfrutan de mini piscina.

È possibile scegliere ville con una o due camere da letto, tutte dotate di spazioso bagno semiaperto e di terrazza. 53 dispongono anche di mini-piscina privata.

A view over the main swimming pool and beach out to sea is available from the Samui Restaurant. Many guests still prefer to have Thai specialties served on the terrace of their villas.

Einen Blick über das Hauptschwimmbad und den Strand aufs Meer bietet das Samui-Restaurant. Viele der Gäste lassen sich aber trotzdem die thailändischen Speisen lieber auf der Terrasse ihrer Villa servieren.

Le restaurant Samui offre une vue sur la piscine principale et la plage, et plus loin sur la mer. De nombreux visiteurs préfèrent tout de même se faire servir les plats thaïlandais à la terrasse de leur villa.

El restaurante Samui ofrece vistas que alcanzan más allá de la piscina principal y la playa hasta el mar. Aún así, algunos de los huéspedes optan por disfrutar de los platos tailandeses servidos en la terraza de su villa.

Dal ristorante Samui si gode della vista sulla piscina principale, sulla spiaggia e sul mare. Molti ospiti preferiscono tuttavia farsi servire le specialità tailandesi sulla terrazza della propria villa.

Evason Hideaway & Six Senses Spa at Ana Mandara

Nha Trang, Vietnam

In the secluded bay of Ninh Van, near to "Vietnam's Nice" Nha Trang, the sanctuary is located in unspoiled nature and accessible by a half-hour boat ride. The 55 villas are spread around the steeply rising slopes, between rough cliff formations, white sandy beach and the protruding coral reef. Guests enjoy a panoramic view across the bay from the terraces belonging to each villa as well as from the villa's baths and bedrooms. The design is best described as luxurious simplicity, with nature playing the leading role.

In der abgeschiedenen Bucht von Ninh Van, nahe dem „Nizza Vietnams" Nha Trang, präsentiert sich das mit einer halbstündigen Bootsfahrt erreichbare Refugium in unverbrauchter Natur. Die 55 Villen liegen verteilt an den steil ansteigenden Hügeln, zwischen schroffen Felsformationen, weißem Sandstrand und dem vorgelagerten Korallenriff. Von den jeweils dazugehörigen Terrassen sowie aus vielen Bädern und Schlafzimmern genießt man einen Panoramablick über die Bucht. Das Design ist am besten mit luxuriöser Schlichtheit beschrieben, bei der die Natur die Hauptrolle spielt.

C'est dans la baie retirée de Ninh Van, à proximité du « Nizza Vietnams » Nha Trang, que se trouve le refuge, accessible en une demi-heure par bateau dans une nature encore vierge. Les 55 villas sont réparties sur les collines escarpées, entre des formations rocheuses abruptes, la plage de sable blanc et la barrière de corail située en amont. Les terrasses attenantes, tout comme les nombreuses piscines et les chambres à coucher, offrent au visiteur une vue panoramique sur la baie. Le design est caractérisé par une simplicité luxueuse dans laquelle le rôle principal revient à la nature.

Engarzado en la escondida bahía de Ninh Van, no lejos de Nha Trang, la "Niza de Vietnam", se encuentra un refugio envuelto por la naturaleza salvaje, al que se accede en media hora de barco. Las 55 villas se dispersan por las colinas escarpadas, entre abruptas formaciones rocosas, una playa de arena blanca y un arrecife de coral. Desde las terrazas y muchos de los baños y dormitorios de las villas se abren vistas panorámicas sobre la bahía. El diseño se define en dos palabras: austeridad lujosa, en la que la naturaleza juega el papel principal.

Nella solitaria baia di Ninh Van, nei pressi di Nha Trang, la "Nizza del Vietnam", nel mezzo di una natura incontaminata, si trova questo rifugio raggiungibile in barca in mezz'ora. Le 55 ville sono sparse sui ripidi pendii delle colline, tra erte formazioni rocciose, spiagge bianche e l'antistante barriera corallina. Dalle terrazze private, dai bagni e dalle camere da letto si può ammirare la baia. La prerogativa del design è una lussuosa semplicità, nella quale la natura è protagonista.

On the outside, the villas appear like purist huts. But the interior takes care of every comfort.

Nach außen wirken die Villen wie puristische Hütten. Ihre Einrichtung lässt jedoch keinen Komfort vermissen.

Les villas font l'effet de huttes puristes. Toutefois leur installation ne manque d'aucun confort.

Hacia el exterior las villas parecen cabañas en estilo purista. Los interiores sin embargo son un derroche de confort.

Le ville hanno esternamente l'aspetto di capanne stilizzate. L'arredamento è però dotato di tutti i comfort.

Dream vistas from the bedroom and bath are inclusive here, no matter whether you are accommodated in a water, beach, rock or hilltop villa, or enjoy a massage in one of the treatment rooms in the 100,000-square foot Six Senses Spa.

Traumausblicke aus dem Schlafzimmer und Bad sind hier inklusive, egal ob man eine Water-, Beach-, Rock- bzw. Hilltop-Villa bewohnt oder sich in einem der Behandlungsräume des 10.000 Quadratmeter großen Six Senses Spa massieren lässt.

Les panoramas de rêve dans la chambre à coucher et dans la piscine sont ici inclus, que l'on réside dans une villa Water, Beach, Rock ou Hilltop ou que l'on se fasse masser dans l'une des pièces destinées aux soins du Six Senses Spa de 10 000 mètres carrés.

Las vistas de ensueño desde el dormitorio y el baño son obligadas, ya se elija una Water, Beach, Rock o Hilltop Villa, o bien se opte por un masaje en uno de los salones de tratamientos que integran los 10.000 metros cuadrados del Six Senses Spa.

Viste da sogno dalla camera da letto o dal bagno sono incluse nei comfort, sia dalle ville situate su acqua, spiaggia, roccia e collina, sia dalle cabine di trattamento della Six Senses Spa, che si estende su un'area di 10.000 metri quadrati.

The Sentosa Resort & Spa

Singapore

Located only ten minutes by car from the center of Singapore, the resort on the outlying island of Sentosa is an attractive alternative to the city-center hotels. The resort's 210 rooms, four villas, restaurants and the Spa Botanica are spread over several buildings in nostalgic colonial style across a park-like site on a slope. From the swimming pool and neighboring Restaurant Cliff, guests have a panoramic vista overlooking the nearby sandy beach and giant harbors.

Nur zehn Autominuten vom Zentrum Singapurs entfernt, ist das auf der vorgelagerten Insel Sentosa gelegene Resort eine attraktive Alternative zu den Hotels in der Stadt. Die 210 Zimmer und vier Villen der Anlage, die Restaurants und das Spa Botanica verteilen sich in mehrere Bauten im nostalgischen Kolonialstil über ein parkartiges Gelände auf einer Anhöhe. Vom Schwimmbad und dem daneben gelegenen Restaurant Cliff bietet sich ein Panoramaausblick auf den nahen Sandstrand und den riesigen Hafen.

À seulement dix minutes en voiture du centre de Singapour, le complexe construit sur l'île de Sentosa situé en amont représente une alternative intéressante aux hôtels situés en ville. Les 210 chambres et quattre villas de l'hôtel, les restaurants et le Spa Botanica sont répartis dans plusieurs édifices au style colonial nostalgique sur un terrain en hauteur rappelant un parc. Dans la piscine et le restaurant Cliff situé à côté, le visiteur profite d'une vue panoramique sur la plage de sable se trouvant à proximité et sur le gigantesque port.

En tan sólo diez minutos en coche desde el centro de Singapur se alcanza la isla Sentosa que alberga el resort y supone una atractiva alternativa a los hoteles de la ciudad. Las 210 habitaciones y cuatro villas, restaurantes y el Spa Botanica están distribuidos en edificios en estilo colonial de toque nostálgico, por un recinto de parque sobre una elevación de terreno. Tanto la piscina como el restaurante anexo, el Cliff, brindan vistas panorámicas a la cercana playa y el inmenso puerto.

A soli dieci minuti di macchina dal centro di Singapore, questo resort situato sull'antistante isola di Sentosa è una magnifica alternativa agli hotel cittadini. Le 210 camere e quattro ville del complesso, i ristoranti e la Spa Botanica sono distribuiti in più edifici in nostalgico stile coloniale, situati in un'area-parco posta su un'altura. Dalla piscina e dall'adiacente ristorante Cliff si gode di una vista panoramica sulla vicina spiaggia sabbiosa e sul grandissimo porto.

A main aim of Australian architect Kerry Hill is to integrate nature into his buildings. Internal and external boundaries are correspondingly fluid.

Ein Anliegen des australischen Architekten Kerry Hill ist es, die Natur in seine Bauten zu integrieren. Entsprechend fließen die Grenzen zwischen innen und außen.

L'un des souhaits de l'architecte australien Kerry Hill est d'intégrer la nature dans ses constructions. C'est pourquoi les limites traversent l'intérieur et l'extérieur.

Para el arquitecto australiano Kerry Hill es fundamental integrar la naturaleza en sus construcciones. Así se difuminan las barreras entre el interior y el exterior.

L'intento dell'architetto australiano Kerry Hill è quello di integrare la natura nei suoi progetti: i confini tra interni ed esterni si fondono armonicamente gli uni negli altri.

Located in a tropical garden and equipped with two private pools, fitness center and teahouse, the Spa Botanica offers almost every imaginable treatment. It is also open to day visitors.

Das in einem tropischen Garten mit zwei eigenen Pools, Fitnesszentrum und Teehaus ausgestatte Spa Botanica bietet nahezu alle denkbaren Behandlungen an. Es ist auch für Tagesbesucher offen.

Le Spa Botanica, aménagé dans un jardin tropical et doté de deux piscines, d'un centre fitness et d'une maison du thé, offre quasiment tous les soins imaginables. Il est également disponible aux visiteurs de jour.

El Spa Botanica, ubicado en un jardín con piscinas propias, gimnasio y casa del té propone casi todo tipo de tratamientos y está también abierto para visitantes de un día.

La Spa Botanica, situata in un giardino tropicale e dotata di due piscine, centro fitness e sala da tè, offre quasi tutti i trattamenti possibili. È aperta anche per visite giornaliere.

Four Seasons Resort Bali at Sayan

Bali, Indonesia

In the highland of Bali near Ubud at a gentle curve of the holy river of Ayung is the setting of one of the most avant-garde hotel buildings of recent years. Cascades of water are everywhere, streams flow through the walkways of the 600-foot long main building, and the guest villas at the riverbank almost sink into the lush rain forest. In the spa, soothing, Ayurvedic treatments are on offer. Only natural ingredients such as sandalwood, flower petals and exotic spices are used.

Im Hochland von Bali nahe Ubud an einer sanften Biegung des heiligen Flusses Ayung liegt einer der avantgardistischsten Hotelbauten der letzten Jahre. Überall finden sich Kaskaden von Wasser, Bäche fließen durch die Gänge des 180 Meter langen Hauptgebäudes, die Gästevillen am Flussufer versinken fast im üppigen Regenwald. Im Spa werden wohltuende ayurvedische Behandlungen verabreicht. Verwendung finden ausschließlich natürliche Ingredienzien wie Sandelholz, Blütenblätter und exotische Gewürze.

C'est dans le haut plateau de Bali près de Ubud, le long d'un doux méandre du fleuve sacré Ayung, que se trouve l'un des édifices les plus avant-gardes de ces dernières années. On rencontre partout des cascades d'eau, des ruisseaux s'écoulent dans les couloirs du bâtiment principal de 180 mètres de hauteur, les villas des visiteurs situées le long de la rive du fleuve s'enfoncent quasiment dans la forêt tropicale luxuriante. Des soins ayurvédiques bienfaisants sont disponibles dans le spa. Seuls des ingrédients naturels tels que le bois de santal, les pétales et les épices exotiques sont utilisés.

En las tierras altas de Bali, cercano a Ubud y ubicada en un suave meandro del río sagrado Ayung, se encuentra una de las construcciones hoteleras más vanguardistas de los últimos años. El lugar está bañado de innumerables cascadas y riachuelos que discurren por los pasillos del edificio de 180 metros. Las villas para los huéspedes a orillas del río se funden en la exuberante selva. El spa brinda tratamientos de bienestar Ayurveda, a base de elementos exclusivamente naturales como madera de sándalo, pétalos de flor y especias exóticas.

Sull'altopiano di Bali, vicino ad Ubud, nel punto in cui il fiume sacro Ayung s'incurva dolcemente, è situato uno degli hotel dal design più avanguardistico degli ultimi anni. Ovunque si trovano cascate d'acqua, ruscelli scorrono attraverso i corridoi dell'edificio principale, lungo 180 metri, mentre le ville degli ospiti sulla riva del fiume spariscono quasi nella rigogliosa foresta tropicale. Nella spa vengono praticati benefici trattamenti ayuverdici, utilizzando esclusivamente ingredienti naturali, come legno di sandalo, petali di fiori ed aromi esotici.

Balinese elements are reflected in the building style of the semi-open spa villas.

Balinesische Elemente spiegeln sich in der Bauweise der halboffenen Spa-Villen wieder.

Les éléments balinais se reflètent dans le style de construction des villas spa semi-ouvertes.

Los elementos balineses se reflejan en la forma de construcción de las villas spa semiabiertas.

Gli elementi caratteristici di Bali si ritrovano nello stile architettonico delle ville della spa, aperte sui lati.

A further 42 villas, each with a private pool, are grouped around the main building with open-air restaurant, bar and 18 suites. The most popular villas are located right on Ayung River.

Um das Hauptgebäude mit Open-Air-Restaurant und Bar sowie 18 Suiten gruppieren sich weitere 42 Villen, alle mit eigenem Pool. Die begehrtesten liegen direkt am Ayung Fluss.

42 villas, comprenant toutes leur propre piscine, sont groupées autour du bâtiment principal avec restaurant en plein air et bar ainsi que 18 suites. Les villas les plus recherchées sont situées directement le long du fleuve Ayung.

Entorno al edificio principal con restaurante al aire libre, bar y 18 suites se reúnen otras 42 villas, todas ellas con piscina propia. Las más solicitadas dan directamente al río Ayung.

Intorno all'edificio principale con ristorante e bar all'aperto sono raggruppate altre 42 ville, tutte con piscina privata. Le più ambite si trovano direttamente sul fiume Ayung.

The Ritz-Carlton Bali Resort & Spa

Bali, Indonesia

Set along the cliffs of Jimbaran peninsula is the location for the luxurious resort with private beach and 18-hole putting course away from the bustle of the tourists. The 375 rooms, suites and villas are scattered about the tropical parkland site, many of them offer a panoramic view across the Indian Ocean. A highlight in terms of contemporary design is the new complex with 38 cliff villas, the restaurants Dava, Martini Bar, pool area and wedding chapel. For their culinary delights guests can choose among four restaurants and three bars.

Entlang der Klippen der Halbinsel Jimbaran gebaut, liegt das luxuriöse Resort mit Privatstrand und 18-Loch Putting Course abseits des touristischen Trubels. Die 375 Zimmer, Suiten und Villen sind verstreut über die tropische Parkanlage, viele von ihnen bieten eine Panoramaaussicht über den Indischen Ozean. In Sachen Design besonders attraktiv ist der neue Komplex der 38 Cliff-Villen mit dem Restaurant Dava und Martini Bar sowie eigener Poollandschaft und Hochzeitskapelle. Kulinarisch haben die Gäste die Auswahl aus vier Restaurants und drei Bars.

C'est le long des rochers de la presqu'île de Jimbaran, loin de l'effervescence touristique, qu'a été aménagé cet ensemble luxueux, avec plage privée et terrain de golf à 18 trous. Les 375 chambres, suites et villas sont éparpillées dans le parc tropical, certaines d'entre elles offrant même une vue panoramique sur l'Océan Indien. Avec le restaurant Dava et le Martini Bar, ainsi que l'agencement superbe de son ensemble de piscines et sa chapelle de mariage, le nouveau complexe de villas aux 38 rochers est particulièrement attractif en matière de design. Pour les repas, les visiteurs ont le choix entre quatre restaurants et trois bars.

Situado en los acantilados de la península de Jimbaran se encuentra el lujoso resort con playa propia y campo de golf de 18 hoyos, completamente al margen del ajetreo turístico. Las 375 habitaciones, villas y suites se dispersan por el parque tropical y muchas de ellas cuentan con vistas panorámicas al Océano Índico. En cuanto al diseño, lo que más destacan son las nuevas 38 villas del acantilado, el restaurante Dava, Martini Bar, el area de la piscina y la capilla de bodas. Para la delicia culinaria los huéspedes pueden escoger entre los cuatro restaurantes y tres bares.

Costruito lungo la scogliera della penisola di Jimbaran, questo lussuoso resort, dotato di spiaggia privata e putting course con 18 buche, sorge lontano dal trambusto turistico. Le 375 camere, suite e ville, molte delle quali con vista panoramica sull'Oceano Indiano, sono sparse nel parco tropicale. Particolarmente attraente dal punto di vista del design è il nuovo complesso che comprende 38 Cliff Ville, il ristorante Dava, il Martini bar, un proprio parco piscina ed una cappella matrimoniale. Per quel che riguarda l'aspetto gastronomico, gli ospiti possono scegliere tra quattro ristoranti e tre bar.

In architectural terms, the resort fluctuates between neo-Baroque Ritz-Carlton tradition and minimalist Bali-modern.

In der Architektur bewegt sich die Anlage zwischen neobarocker Ritz-Carlton-Tradition und minimalistischem Bali modern.

Au niveau architectural, le complexe évolue entre la tradition du Ritz-Carlton néo-baroque et le Bali minimaliste moderne.

En el plano arquitectónico el lugar combina la tradición neobarroca del Ritz-Carlton y las líneas modernas y minimalistas balinesas.

Architettonicamente il complesso oscilla tra la tradizione neobarocca propria del Ritz-Carlton e lo stile moderno-minimalista di Bali.

A signature feature of the 95,000-square foot spa is the thalassotherapy, with a 7,000-square foot salt-water pool, internationally the largest of its kind.

Eine Besonderheit des 9000 Quadratmeter großen Spa ist die Thalassotherapie mit einem 650 Quadratmeter großen Salzwasserpool, dem weltgrößten seiner Art.

La particularité du spa de 9000 mètres carrés est la thalassothérapie avec sa piscine d'eau salée de 650 mètres carrés, la plus grande au monde dans son genre.

Una de las exclusividades del spa de 9000 metros cuadrados es la talasoterapia, con piscina de agua salada de 650 metros cuadrados, la más grande de su categoría.

Una particolarità della spa di 9000 metri quadrati è la talassoterapia, con una piscina d'acqua salata di 650 metri quadrati, la più grande al mondo di questo tipo.

Voyages Bedarra Island

North Queensland, Australia

This granite-cliff idyll, with its concealed sandy bays, crystal-clear water and a tropical climate is right at the top of the list of celebrities' favorites. 14 villas and two glass pavilions in the style of futuristic pre-fabricated houses are well hidden under the leafy canopy of the rain forest and they maintain the greatest possible distance from each other. Here, everything is tailored to privacy, the masseur visits the guests, and the butler provides the same service with the meals. Just if you are curious to look who is curious too, you can also dine al fresco on the restaurant's terrace.

Dieses Idyll aus Granitfelsen, versteckten Sandbuchten, glasklarem Wasser und tropischem Klima steht bei prominenten Persönlichkeiten ganz oben auf der Beliebtheitsskala. 14 Villen und zwei verglaste Pavillons im Stil zukunftsweisender Fertighäuser, liegen gut getarnt unter dem Blätterdach des Regenwalds und halten den größtmöglichen Abstand voneinander. Alles ist auf Intimität getrimmt, der Masseur kommt hier zu den Gästen, der Butler mit dem Essen ebenso. Es sei denn man ist neugierig, wer sonst noch neugierig ist, und diniert al fresco auf dem Terrassenrestaurant.

Cette idylle de rochers de granite, de baies de sable cachées, d'eau translucide et de climat tropical rencontre un grand succès parmi les personnalités célèbres. 14 villas et deux pavillons vitrés dans le style de maisons préfabriquées futuristes sont camouflées à la perfection sous le toit en feuillage de la forêt tropicale et sont espacées de la plus grande distance possible. L'accent est mis entièrement sur l'intimité : le masseur rend visite aux clients et il en est de même pour le serveur avec le repas. À moins que l'on ne fasse preuve de curiosité et que l'on dîne al fresco au restaurant de la terrasse.

Un idilio de rocas de granito, bahías escondidas de arena fina, agua cristalina y clima tropical que se ha convertido en uno de los destinos preferidos de los famosos. 14 villas y dos pabellones acristalados con un estilo de casa prefabricada futurista, al remanso de un techo de selva virgen y a la mayor distancia posible unas de otras. Todo está enfocado a la intimidad; aquí tanto el masajista como el mayordomo con la comida van a los huéspedes, y no al contrario. A no ser que la curiosidad incite a cenar al fresco en la terraza del restaurante.

Questo idillio di rocce di granito, baie sabbiose nascoste, acqua chiarissima e clima tropicale è il posto preferito dalle celebrità. 14 ville e due padiglioni a vetri, simili a case prefabbricate di stampo futuristico, si trovano accuratamente nascosti sotto il tetto di foglie della foresta tropicale, ben distanziati gli uni dagli altri. Tutto è volto alla difesa della privacy: il massaggiatore e il maggiordomo vanno a domicilio dagli ospiti. A meno che – spinti dalla curiosità – non si desideri cenare al fresco nel ristorante con terrazza.

Set a little apart from the villas that were built first are the two hypermodern wood-glass pavilions with their mini-pool docked alongside.

Etwas abseits von den zuerst erbauten Villen liegen die beiden hypermodernen Holz-Glas-Pavillons mit ihrem angedockten Minipool.

Les deux pavillons hypermodernes en bois et en verre avec leur minipiscine attenante sont placés quelque peu à l'écart des villas construites en premier lieu.

Los dos supermodernos pabellones de cristal y madera y la mini piscina adjunta están ubicados a cierta distancia de las primeras villas que se construyeron.

Poco distante dalle prime ville si trovano i due modernissimi padiglioni in legno e vetro con minipiscina annessa.

A secure place for inspiration. At full capacity, a maximum of 34 guests are accommodated above the bay of Wedgerock.

Ein sicherer Ort zur Inspiration. Bei voller Belegung versammeln sich oberhalb der Bucht von Wedgerock maximal nur 34 Gäste.

Un lieu sûr voué à l'inspiration. Lorsque l'hôtel est complet, ce sont au maximum 34 clients qui sont réunis au-dessus de la baie de Wedgerock.

La inspiración está asegurada. No son más de 34 huéspedes los que pueden disfrutar de este rincón sobre la bahía de Wedgerock.

Un posto sicuro per trovare ispirazione. Quando è al completo, l'hotel sulla baia di Wedgerock conta al massimo 34 ospiti.

Voyages Bedarra Island *North Queensland, Australia*   173

Post Ranch Inn

Big Sur, California

Set 1,200 feet above the sea is California's secret laid-back luxury resort. It is both modern and rustic, as well as environmentally aware. Half of the inn's 30 rooms overlook the mountains; the rest offer a view of the Pacific Ocean. The stylish accommodations consist mainly of separate houses perched up on the cliff like tree-house dwellings, with a cozy fireplace, spa tub, and private deck. The hotel offers yoga in a circular canvas yurt daily, as well as lectures on stargazing.

360 Meter über dem Meer befindet sich Kaliforniens verstecktes Luxusresort. Es ist sowohl modern und schlicht, als auch umweltgerecht. Von der Hälfte der 30 Zimmer bietet sich ein Ausblick auf das Gebirge, die anderen überblicken den Pazifik. Der Gast wohnt in stilvollen Einzelhäusern, die sich wie Baumhäuser auf den Klippen drängen, jedes mit offenem Kamin, einem Spa und privater Veranda. Das Hotel bietet tägliche Yogakurse in einem runden Leinwandzelt an, dazu Kurse in Sternenbeobachtung.

Le complexe de luxe caché de la Californie est situé à 360 mètres au-dessus du niveau de la mer. Il est à la fois moderne et rustique, mais tient également compte de l'environnement. La moitié des 30 chambres offre une vue sur le massif montagneux, l'autre moitié sur l'océan Pacifique. Le visiteur réside dans une maison individuelle stylée qui s'accroche aux rochers telle une cabane dans un arbre. Elles disposent toutes d'une cheminée agréable, d'un spa et d'une véranda privée. Le hôtel propose des cours de yoga quotidiens dans une tente ronde en toile, ainsi que des cours pour apprendre à observer les étoiles.

A 360 metros sobre el mar se encuentra el resort de lujo más escondido de California. Además de estar dotado de un aire moderno y austero al mismo tiempo se jacta de ser respetuoso con el medio ambiente. De las 30 habitaciones, la mitad ofrece una panorámica a las montañas y la otra mitad lanza la vista al Pacífico. Para el huésped se han concebido casas individuales cargadas de estilo que se asoman al acantilado, dotadas de una acogedora chimenea, spa y terraza privada. El spa del hotel propone cursos de yoga diarios en una tienda circular de tela de lino, así como cursos de observación de las estrellas.

Questo appartato resort di lusso californiano si trova a 360 metri sul livello del mare. Moderno e semplice al tempo stesso, è stato costruito nel rispetto dell'ambiente. Una metà delle 30 camere ha vista sulle montagne, l'altra si affaccia sul Pacifico. L'ospite abita in raffinate villette, incastonate tra gli scogli come casette sugli alberi, tutte con accogliente camino, spa e veranda privata. L'hotel propone corsi giornalieri di yoga in una tenda rotonda di lino ed, inoltre, corsi di osservazione astronomica.

Amenities include in-room spa treatments from dawn until midnight, and a marble Jacuzzi with wide-angle mountain and ocean views.

Zu den Annehmlichkeiten gehören Spa-Behandlungen in den Suiten vom Morgengrauen bis Mitternacht und ein marmorner Jacuzzi mit Panoramablick auf die Berge und den Ozean.

Parmi les activités offertes, des soins de spa prodigués dans les suites de l'aube jusqu'à minuit ainsi qu'un jacuzzi en marbre offrant une vue fantastique sur les montagnes et l'océan.

Entre los servicios se incluyen los tratamientos del spa en las suites desde primera hora de la mañana hasta medianoche, además de un jacuzzi de mármol con vistas a las montañas y al océano.

I comfort comprendono trattamenti spa dall'alba a mezzanotte nelle suite ed una Jacuzzi di marmo con ampia vista sulle montagne e sull'Oceano.

Splurge on one of the luxurious grass-roofed suites tucked away into the landscape, with stunning ocean views and majestic treescapes.

Geben Sie ihr Geld für eine der luxuriösen, grasgedeckten Suiten aus, die sich in die Landschaft einschmiegen und atemberaubende Blicke über das Meer und die majestätische Baumlandschaft erlauben.

Dépensez votre argent pour l'une des suites luxueuses et recouvertes de pelouse qui se fondent dans le paysage et vous offrent une vue splendide sur la mer et le paysage majestueux formé par les arbres.

Despréndase del dinero en una de las lujosas suites cubiertas de hierba, perfectamente integrada en el paisaje, con vistas al mar y a un majestuoso paisaje de bosque.

Vale la pena spendere i propri soldi per una delle lussuose suite coperte d'erba tuffate nel paesaggio da cui si può godere della magnifica vista sul mare e sulla maestosa vegetazione arborea.

176   Post Ranch Inn *Big Sur, California*

The Ritz-Carlton South Beach
Miami, Florida

The lushly landscaped Ritz-Carlton is a complete restoration of the original Morris Lapidus-designed landmark hotel DiLido. Located in the heart of the historic Art Deco district, it is a short walk from Lincoln Road, a thriving pedestrian esplanade of countless dining and shopping options. Amenities include more than what one would expect from a five-star hotel, like a 24-hour butler, a poolside DJ, a sunset synchronized-swimming show, and a beach club on its own private shoreline.

Für das landschaftlich reizvoll gelegene Ritz-Carlton wurde das wegweisende, von Morris Lapidus gestaltete DiLido Hotel vollständig restauriert. Es befindet sich im Herzen des historischen Art-déco-Bezirkes, nur wenige Schritte von der Lincoln Road, der lebendigen Fußgängerpromenade mit ihren unzähligen Einkaufs- und Ausgehangeboten, entfernt. Zu den Annehmlichkeiten, die ein Fünf-Sterne-Hotel zu bieten hat, kommen noch ein 24-Stunden-Butler, ein Pool-DJ, Synchronschwimmshows bei Sonnenuntergang und ein Beachclub am Privatstrand hinzu.

DiLido, l'hôtel innovant conçu par Morris Lapidus, a été entièrement rénové pour accueillir l'hôtel Ritz-Carlton dans un paysage somptueux. Il est situé au cœur de l'arrondissement historique Art Déco, à quelques pas seulement de la Lincoln Road, zone piétonne trépidante qui recèle de nombreux restaurants et une multitude d'endroits pour sortir. Parmi les commodités qu'offre un hôtel cinq étoiles viennent encore s'ajouter les services d'un maître d'hôtel pendant 24 heures, un DJ pour la piscine, des shows de natation synchronisée au coucher du soleil et un beachclub sur la plage privée.

Para construir este Ritz-Carlon ubicado en un paisaje natural exuberante se restauró por completo el hotel DiLido, obra modelo de Morris Lapidus. El hotel se encuentra en el corazón del barrio histórico Art Deco, a unos pasos de la Lincoln Road, un agitado paseo peatonal que propone innumerables comercios y lugares de ocio. Entre los servicios que ofrece el hotel de cinco estrellas destacan: mayordomo las 24 horas del día, discjockey en la piscina, un espectáculo al atardecer de natación sincronizada y Beachclub con playa privada.

Per il Ritz-Carlton, situato in uno splendido paesaggio, è stato completamente restaurato il DiLido Hotel, precursore nel suo genere, progettato da Morris Lapidus. Esso si trova nel cuore dello storico quartiere Art Deco, a pochi passi da Lincoln Road, l'affollata area pedonale con innumerevoli negozi e locali. Tra i comfort offerti da questo hotel a cinque stelle sono compresi un maggiordomo 24 ore su 24, un DJ presso la piscina, uno spettacolo di nuoto sincronizzato al tramonto ed un beach club sulla spiaggia privata.

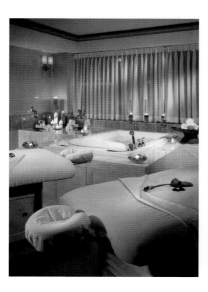

A world-class spa featuring La Maison de Beauté Carita, the first signature spa outside of Paris, and the largest spa on Miami Beach.

Ein Spa der Weltklasse mit der La Maison de Beauté Carita, dem ersten Spa des Instituts außerhalb von Paris und dem größten in Miami Beach.

Un Spa de classe mondiale avec La Maison de Beauté Carita, le premier de cet institut hors de Paris et le plus important à Miami Beach.

Un spa de nivel internacional con La Maison de Beauté Carita, el primer spa de la casa fuera de París y el mayor de Miami Beach.

Una spa di prim'ordine con La Maison de Beauté Carita, la prima spa dell'istituto dopo Parigi e la più grande di Miami Beach.

376 guest rooms *feature the plush interiors of a luxury yacht. The lobby is a perfect replica of the original hotel, and as stylish today as it must have been in 1953.*

Die 376 Gästeräume *überzeugen mit dem exklusiven Interieur einer Luxusyacht. Die Lobby ist ein perfekter Nachbau des Originalhotels und heute noch so stilvoll wie sie 1953 gewesen sein dürfte.*

Les 376 pièces *destinées aux visiteurs séduisent avec leur intérieur somptueux, semblable à celui d'un yacht de luxe. Le lobby est une réplique parfaite de celui de l'hôtel d'origine et a aujourd'hui autant de style qu'en 1953.*

Las 376 habitaciones *convencen con sus interiores distinguidos de yate de lujo. El vestíbulo es una copia del hotel original, cargado de tanto estilo como en 1953.*

Le 376 camere, *dai raffinati interni che ricordano quelli di uno yacht di lusso, incontrano il gusto degli ospiti. La lobby è stata costruita su perfetta imitazione dell'hotel originale ed ha oggi la stessa raffinatezza che la caratterizzava già nel 1953.*

Mandarin Oriental Miami

Miami, Florida

Each of the 329 residential-style rooms on the 44-acre island of Brickell Key offers a breathtaking waterfront view of Biscayne Bay. Each luxurious room is an elegant haven that evokes a tranquil feel. Guests can indulge in any of the traditional Thai and Ayurvedic treatments in the 15,000 square-foot spa, or on a cushioned bed in a cabaña on the private white sand beach club. The super attentive staff is trained in Asia to demonstrate the hotel's unique brand of impeccable service.

Aus jedem der 329 Zimmer und Suiten auf der 18 Hektar großen Insel Brickell Key bietet sich ein atemberaubender Blick über die Biscayne Bay. Jeder der luxuriösen Räume gleicht einem eleganten Zufluchtsort, der die Atmosphäre entspannter Gelassenheit ausstrahlt. Die Gäste können im 1400 Quadratmeter großen Spa alle möglichen Thai- oder Ayurveda-Behandlungen genießen oder auf einem Polsterbett in einer Cabaña am weißen Hotelstrand ausspannen. Das extrem aufmerksame Personal wurde in Asien geschult, um dem Ruf der Hotels von perfektem Service gerecht zu werden.

Les 329 chambres et suites sur l'île de 18 hectares de Brickell Key offrent chacune une vue sur la Biscayne Bay à en couper le souffle. Chaque pièce luxueuse ressemble à un port élégant qui dégage une atmosphère de tranquillité et de calme. Les visiteurs peuvent bénéficier de soins thaïlandais ou ayurvédiques dans le spa de 1400 mètres carrés ou décompresser sur un lit matelassé dans une cabaña sur la plage blanche de l'hôtel. Le personnel extrêmement attentif a été formé en Asie, conformément à la très bonne réputation dont jouit cet hôtel en matière de service.

Desde cada una de las 329 habitaciones y suites de la isla de 18 hectáreas Brickell Key se obtiene una espectacular vista sobre Biscayne Bay. Las lujosas estancias se asemejan a un elegante refugio y emanan un ambiente de serenidad. Los huéspedes pueden disfrutar en los 1400 metros cuadrados del spa de los tratamientos tailandeses y Ayurveda, o bien relajarse en las tumbonas tapizadas de las cabañas ubicadas en la blanca playa del hotel. El extremadamente atento personal ha sido formado en Asia con objeto de ofrecer a los huéspedes un perfecto servicio, que de testimonio de la fama que sustenta el hotel.

Da ognuna delle 329 camere e suite di Brickell Key, un'isola di 18 ettari, si gode di una meravigliosa vista sulla Biscayne Bay. Ogni camera è simile ad un elegante rifugio che irradia un'atmosfera di rilassante tranquillità. Nella spa, di 1400 metri quadrati, gli ospiti possono rilassarsi con trattamenti tailandesi o Ayurveda o godere il sole sulla spiaggia bianca privata, distesi su un lettino in una cabaña. Il personale, particolarmente attento, è stato addestrato in Asia, e fa del perfetto servizio dell'hotel un lusso all'altezza della propria fama.

*A **perfect spa retreat** for the person who wants to escape from the South Beach spotlight, but still needs to be close to the Miami madness.*

*Das **ideale Refugium** für jeden, der den Lichtern von South Beach entfliehen möchte, ohne auf die Nähe zum verrückten Miami verzichten zu wollen.*

*Le **refuge** parfait pour celui qui souhaite fuir les lumières de South Beach sans renoncer à la proximité de l'ambiance trépidante de Miami.*

*El **refugio** perfecto para quienes deseen escapar de las luces de South Beach sin por ello renunciar a la proximidad de la frenética Miami.*

*Il **rifugio** perfetto per chiunque voglia fuggire dalle luci di South Beach senza rinunciare alla vicinanza della pazza Miami.*

The interiors combine modern touches with exotic Asian elements, such as the bamboo hardwood floors to the Spanish marble in the bathrooms.

In den Innenräumen wird modernen Stil mit asiatischen Elementen kombiniert, in den Bädern beispielsweise Fußböden aus Bambus mit spanischem Marmor.

Un mélange de styles avec des éléments modernes et asiatiques règne dans les pièces intérieures, les sols des salles de bain en bambou sont par exemple associés à du marbre espagnol.

En los interiores domina una mezcla de estilos cargados de elementos modernos y asiáticos: en los baños, por ejemplo, suelos de bambú con mármol español.

Gli interni sono arredati con una combinazione di elementi moderni ed orientali: nei bagni, ad esempio, i pavimenti di bambù incontrano il marmo spagnolo.

Parrot Cay
Turks & Caicos Islands, West Indies

Life as usually known will cease to exist in this fashionable hideaway set on a private, 1000-acre island. 60 guest rooms combine Caribbean minimalism with Balinese chic. Ring and a butler will fulfill any whim, from scheduling a spa treatment in a very own private cottage, or arranging for a delicacy to be flown to the island. Feel like a castaway on the dazzling three-mile-long powdered beach. A perfect retreat for those seeking natural beauty, and evenings lit only by the moon and stars.

In diesem extravaganten Hideaway auf einer privaten, 400 Hektar großen Insel verblasst das alltägliche Leben. In den 60 Gästezimmern geht karibischer Minimalismus eine innige Verbindung mit balinesischem Chic ein. Gleich welchen Wunsch man dem Butler auch anträgt – eine Spa-Behandlung in einem speziellen Cottage, eine besondere Delikatesse vom Festland – er wird erfüllt. Fühlen Sie sich wie ein Schiffsbrüchiger auf einem fast 5 Kilometer langen, feinsandigen Strand. Wer Naturschönheiten und Abende sucht, die nur von Mond und Sternen erhellt werden, ist hier richtig.

Dans ce Hideaway extravagant sur une île privée de 400 hectares, la vie quotidienne perd de sa couleur. Dans les 60 chambres destinées aux visiteurs, le minimalisme des Caraïbes s'unit étroitement au chic balinais. Quel que soit le souhait dont vous ferez part au maître d'hôtel (soins de spa dans un cottage spécial, spécialité particulière du continent), il sera réalisé. Mettez-vous dans la peau d'un naufragé sur une longue plage de sable fin de 5 kilomètres. Ceux qui recherchent les beautés naturelles et aiment les soirées éclairées uniquement par la lune et les étoiles seront ici à la bonne adresse.

En este extravagante refugio en una isla privada de 400 hectáreas la rutina se esfuma. Las 60 habitaciones son una fusión del minimalismo del Caribe y el refinamiento de Bali. Pídaselo al mayordomo y sus deseos serán concedidos, ya se trate de un tratamiento spa en una cabaña adaptada para ello, o bien de cualquier exquisitez culinaria traída de tierra firme. Siéntase como un náufrago en la playa de arena fina de casi 5 kilómetros. Quienes busquen belleza natural y noches iluminadas sólo por la luna y las estrellas, han llegado aquí a su destino.

In questo stravagante hideaway situato su un'isola privata di 400 ettari, la vita d'ogni giorno impallidisce. Nelle 60 camere, il minimalismo caraibico si sposa con la raffinatezza di Bali. Qualsiasi desiderio venga espresso al maggiordomo – un trattamento spa in uno speciale cottage, una particolare prelibatezza dalla terra ferma – esso viene esaudito. Qui ci si sente come naufraghi approdati su una spiaggia di sabbia finissima lunga quasi 5 chilometri: il luogo ideale per chi cerca bellezze naturali e serate rischiarate soltanto dalla luna e dalle stelle.

White muslin curtains envelop the four-poster beds, and each of the 60 villas have a private terrace with a rattan chaise facing the azure waters of the ocean.

Weiße Vorhänge aus Musselin hüllen die Himmelbetten ein; zu jeder der 60 Gästevillen gehört eine private Terrasse mit Rattanliege, um den azurblauen Ozean zu genießen.

Des rideaux blancs en mousseline enveloppent les lits à baldaquin ; chacune des 60 villas destinées aux visiteurs possède une terrasse privée avec chaise longue en rotin de façon à profiter de l'océan azur bleu.

Cortinas blancas de muselina cubren la cama con dosel. Las 60 villas cuentan con terraza privada y tumbonas de ratán que invitan a disfrutar del azul del océano.

Tende bianche di mussola incorniciano i letti a baldacchino; di ognuna delle 60 ville fa parte una terrazza privata con divano di rattan, per ammirare l'azzurro dell'Oceano.

Striking lost edge pool is a triumph of illusion, merging with the ocean. The beachfront villas have a soothing Asian feel, and smaller rooms overlook blooming gardens.

Der geschwungene Pool scheint in perfekter Illusion mit dem Meer zu verschmelzen. Die Villen am Strand atmen asiatisches Flair, während sich kleinere Räume auf blühende Gärten öffnen.

La piscine arquée semble se fondre dans la mer avec une illusion parfaite. Les villas construites le long de la plage dégagent un flair asiatique alors que les plus petites pièces s'ouvrent sur des jardins en fleur.

La sinuosa piscina crea la perfecta ilusión de fundirse con el mar. Las villas de la playa respiran el encanto asiático mientras que pequeñas estancias se abren a jardines exuberantes.

La sinuosa piscina sembra fondersi letteralmente con il mare. Le ville sulla spiaggia hanno fascino orientale, mentre le stanze più piccole si aprono su giardini fioriti.

Carlisle Bay

Antigua, West Indies

Located on a secluded beach with a backdrop of rainforests and rolling hills, the resort daringly eschews everything colonial by designing subdued basic interiors to draw attention to the captivating colors of the blooming exotic gardens and frothy sea. Guest rejuvenate at the Amrita Spa in a private villa on an Asian daybed on their very own sundeck. For that extra urban touch, there are in-room espresso machines, a pool with semi-submerged sun loungers, and a 45-seat cinema showing movies every night.

Dieses Resort an einem versteckten Strand vor Regenwäldern und sanften Hügeln verzichtet ganz bewusst auf koloniale Versatzstücke. Stattdessen lenkt das angenehm unterkühlte Design der Innenräume die gesamte Aufmerksamkeit auf die leuchtenden Farben der exotischen Blumengärten und die schäumende See. Die Gäste dürfen sich nach dem Besuch des Amrita Spa verjüngt fühlen, wenn sie das eigene Sonnendeck auf einem asiatischen Tagesbett genießen. Für städtisches Ambiente sorgen Espressomaschinen in jedem Raum, ein Pool mit halb versunkenen Sonnenliegen und ein Kino mit 45 Plätzen, das jeden Abend Filme zeigt.

Ce complexe aménagé sur une plage cachée devant la forêt tropicale et de douces collines renonce volontairement au décor mobile colonial. Au lieu de cela, le design agréablement glacial des pièces intérieures dirige toute l'attention sur les couleurs lumineuses des jardins de fleurs exotiques et la mer moutonneuse. Après s'être rendu dans l'Amrita Spa, le visiteur se sentira rajeuni lorsqu'il profitera de son deck de soleil personnel, allongé sur un lit de jour asiatique. L'ambiance urbaine est garantie par des machines à expresso dans chaque pièce, une piscine avec chaises longues à moitié immergées et un cinéma de 45 places dans lequel un film est programmé chaque soir.

Un resort ubicado en una playa escondida ante un escenario de selva y suaves colinas que renuncia intencionadamente a los motivos coloniales. En su lugar, el centro de atención se dirige hacia el exótico jardín de flores y a la suavidad del mar. Los huéspedes se sentirán rejuvenecidos tras una visita al Amrita Spa, en el que disfrutarán de una cubierta para tomar el sol propia en una tumbona asiática. El toque urbano lo proporcionan las máquinas de expreso disponibles en cada habitación, la piscina con tumbonas en el agua y un cine de 45 plazas que proyecta películas todas las tardes.

Questo resort situato su una spiaggia nascosta sullo sfondo della foresta tropicale e di dolci colline rinuncia completamente ad elementi di stile coloniale. Il design degli interni, raffinato e discreto, attira invece l'attenzione sui colori sgargianti dei giardini esotici e sul mare spumeggiante. Dopo una visita all'Amrita Spa ci si sente ringiovaniti, ed è ancora più piacevole prendere il sole sulla propria terrazza distesi su un lettino asiatico. Macchine per fare l'espresso in ogni camera, una piscina con brandine semi-immerse ed un cinema con 45 posti, aperto ogni sera, non fanno mancare nessuna delle comodità cittadine.

The timeless design combines a cool classy minimalism with the Japanese decorative ideal of perfection, with white walls and weathered wood.

Das zeitlose Design setzt auf kühlen, klassischen Minimalismus und das japanische Ideal von Perfektion — weiße Wände und wettergegerbtes Holz.

Le design intemporel mise sur le minimalisme froid et classique ainsi que sur l'idéal japonais de la perfection : murs blancs et bois tanné par le temps.

El diseño intemporal se apoya en un minimalismo clásico y frío y en el ideal japonés de la perfección, que se expresa en paredes blancas y madera curtida.

Il design atemporale è una combinazione di minimalismo classico e discreto e dell'ideale giapponese di perfezione — pareti bianche e legno duro.

Each of the 88 suites have a terrace that overlooks stunning views, complete with a hardwood daybed and fluttering voile curtains for added privacy.

Jede der 88 Suiten hat eine Terrasse, von der sich fantastische Ausblicke bieten, dazu Tagesbetten aus Hartholz und wehende Voilevorhänge, die Privatheit garantieren.

Les 88 suites disposent chacune d'une terrasse offrant des panoramas superbes ainsi que de lits de jour en bois dur et de voilages vaporeux qui garantissent le respect du domaine privé.

Las 88 suites disponen de una terraza abierta a las fabulosas vistas, con tumbonas de madera dura y vaporosas cortinas que garantizan privacidad.

Le 88 suite hanno tutte una terrazza con splendida vista, divani di legno duro e tendaggi vaporosi, che garantiscono intimità.

194   Carlisle Bay *Antigua, West Indies*

The vast church-like lobby is flanked with discreet tinkling fountains and lily ponds. The futuristic, Lucite library has shelves back-lit in Day-Glo colors.

Die großzügige, kirchenartige Lobby wird von leise plätschernden Brunnen und Seerosenteichen gesäumt. Die Plexiglas-Regale in der futuristischen Bibliothek werden von hinten mit farbigem Neonlicht beleuchtet.

Le vaste lobby rappelant une église est bordé par des fontaines au clapotis léger et des étangs de nénuphars. Les étagères en plexiglas de la bibliothèque futuriste sont rétroéclairées par un néon de couleur.

Un amplio vestíbulo que se asemeja a una iglesia y está salpicado de fuentes y estanques con nenúfar. Las estanterías de plexiglás de la futurista biblioteca están iluminadas por detrás con multicolores luces de neón.

La spaziosa lobby, che ricorda l'architettura di una chiesa, è circondata da fontane gorgoglianti e da stagni di ninfee. Gli scaffali in plexiglas della futuristica biblioteca sono illuminati dal retro con luci al neon colorate.

Raffles Resort Canouan Island

St. Vincent & The Grenadines, West Indies

Luxurious villas in terra-cotta pink protrude out from the hillside, overlooking the largest coral reefs in the Caribbean. Lounge in luxury next to the longest fresh water pool in the region, or on the secluded beaches that surround this 1,000-acre private island. Indulge yourself at the Amrita Spa in one of the ten thatched-roof villas terraced into the hillside, or try a massage in a treatment room with glass-bottom floors that float over water for a soothing natural aquarium show below.

Luxuriöse Villen in rosafarbener Terrakotta blicken von einem Hügel auf die größten Korallenriffe in der Karibik. Genießen Sie den Luxus am längsten Süßwasserpool der Region oder an einem der einsamen Strände, die diese 400 Hektar große, private Insel säumen. Lassen Sie sich in dem Amrita Spa in einer der zehn strohgedeckten, in den Hang gebauten Villen verwöhnen oder genießen Sie eine Massage in einem Raum mit Glasboden direkt über dem Wasser, der Sie in ein natürliches Aquarium blicken lässt.

De la colline, les villas luxueuses en terre cuite rose offrent une vue sur les plus grandes barrières de corail des Caraïbes. Profitez du luxe offert par la piscine d'eau douce la plus longue de la région ou de l'une des plages isolées qui bordent cette île privée de 400 hectares. Dans l'Amrita Spa, faites-vous dorloter dans l'une des dix villas construites sur le versant ou profitez d'un massage dans une pièce dont le sol en verre est posé directement au-dessus de l'eau et laissez-vous envoûter par l'aquarium naturel sous vos pieds.

Las lujosas villas en terracota rosa se asoman desde una colina al mayor arrecife de coral del Caribe. Disfrute del lujo en la piscina de agua dulce más grande de la región o en una de las escondidas playas que rodean esta isla privada de 400 hectáreas. Déjese cuidar en el Amrita Spa, ubicado en una de las diez villas con tejado de paja apoyadas en la ladera, o bien disfrute de un masaje en una sala con suelo de cristal que permite extasiarse con el acuario natural.

Ville lussuose in terracotta rosa si affacciano da una collina sui più grandi banchi corallini dei Carabi. Gli ospiti possono godere di questo lusso ai bordi della piscina d'acqua dolce più lunga della regione o su una delle spiagge isolate che circondano quest'isola privata della superficie di 400 ettari. L'Amrita Spa vizia gli ospiti in una delle dieci ville dal tetto di paglia adagiate sul pendio; l'alternativa è concedersi un massaggio in una sala con pavimento di vetro direttamente sull'acqua, lasciandosi incantare dall'acquario naturale sottostante.

*156 **suites are** set amphitheater-style amid tropical gardens, with private patios looking into a breathtaking panorama of the protected Carenage Bay.*

*156 **Suiten sind** wie in einem Amphitheater zwischen tropischen Gärten platziert. Von privaten Patios bietet sich das atemberaubende Panorama der geschützten Carenage Bay dar.*

*Les 156 **suites** ont été réparties entre les jardins tropicaux comme dans un amphithéâtre. Les patios privés offrent un panorama à en couper le souffle sur la Carenage Bay protégée.*

*156 **suites** se ensamblan entre jardines tropicales como si de un anfiteatro se tratase. Desde los patios privados se divisa un panorama espectacular a la bahía protegida de Carenage Bay.*

*156 **suite** sono situate tra giardini tropicali come in un anfiteatro. Dai patii privati si gode di uno splendido panorama sulla Carenage Bay, un'area protetta.*

Visitors indulge their taste buds in any of the seven award-winning restaurants where fresh ingredients, and top chefs, have been flown in to turn out first-rate cuisine.

Besucher können ihre Geschmackssinne in sieben preisgekrönten Restaurants verwöhnen lassen. Spitzengastronomie garantieren die eingeflogenen frischen Zutaten und ebenfalls eingeflogenen Küchenchefs.

Sept excellents restaurants mettent à l'honneur les sens gustatifs des visiteurs. Les ingrédients frais et les chefs cuisiniers sont dépêchés par avion afin d'offrir une cuisine de qualité supérieure.

Los visitantes tienen la posibilidad de deleitarse en cualquiera de los siete fabulosos restaurantes, hasta los que se traen tanto los productos frescos como el jefe de cocina para garantizar una cocina de élite.

Gli ospiti possono deliziare il palato in sette ottimi ristoranti. La freschezza degli ingredienti e l'abilità degli chef de cuisine — sia gli uni sia gli altri trasportati fin qui in aereo — garantiscono una gastronomia di prim'ordine.

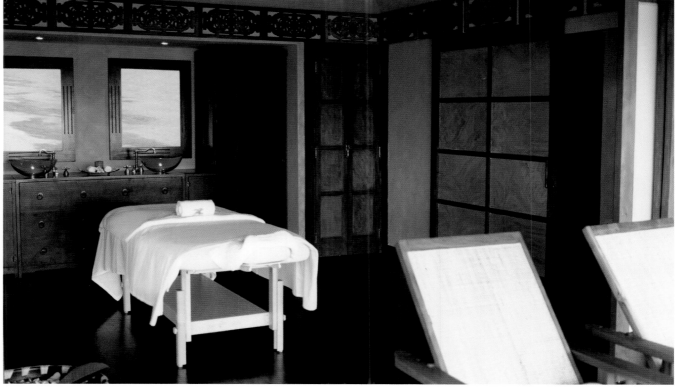

Four Seasons Resort Costa Rica at Peninsula Papagayo

Peninsula Papagayo, Costa Rica

Every suite in this eco-tourist heaven is built into the hillside to blend into the environment with paint color that was computer generated from samples of mud and local trees. The two-level 16,000-square-foot spa is the perfect stop after venturing into the natural attractions of rain forests, volcanoes, and national parks, with beautifully lit private spa rooms that offer treatments unique to Costa Rica, such as mineral-rich rainforest muds taken from the nearby Osa Peninsula.

Jede Suite in diesem Paradies für Ökotouristen ist in die Hügellandschaft eingebettet und verschmilzt mit der Umgebung. Dafür sorgen die computergenerierten Anstriche, die sich an den Erdetönen und den Farben der heimischen Bäume orientieren. Der zweistöckige Spa bietet auf 1500 Quadratmeter Entspannung nach Exkursionen zu den Naturattraktionen des Regenwaldes, der Vulkane und Nationalparks. In sanft beleuchteten Räumen werden Behandlungen angeboten, die einzigartig sind für Costa Rica, etwa mineralreiche Schlammpackungen aus dem Regenwald der nahen Osa-Halbinsel.

Chaque suite de ce paradis pour touristes écologistes est intégrée dans le paysage de collines et se fond dans cet environnement. Les couleurs ont été générées par ordinateur en fonction des teintes de la terre et des arbres locaux. Le spa de deux étages offre sur 1500 mètres carrés la relaxation méritée après les excursions au cours desquelles le visiteur aura découvert le spectacle naturel de la forêt tropicale, des volcans et des parcs nationaux. Des soins spécifiques au Costa Rica vous seront proposés dans les pièces privées du spa éclairées d'une lumière douce, comme par exemple des enveloppes de boue riches en minéraux provenant de la forêt tropicale de la presqu'île Osa se trouvant à proximité.

Cada suite de este paraíso para eco turistas está insertada en el paisaje de colinas fundiéndose con el entorno. Los colores, orientados en los tonos tierra y los árboles autóctonos han sido generados por ordenador. El spa de dos plantas y 1500 metros cuadrados otorga el descanso merecido tras las excursiones a los espectáculos naturales que ofrecen la selva, los volcanes y los parques nacionales. En las estancias privadas fabulosamente iluminadas se dan tratamientos únicos en Costa Rica, como los baños de barro ricos en minerales de la selva provenientes de la vecina península de Osa.

Tutte le suite di questo paradiso per ecoturisti sono incastonate nel paesaggio collinare e si fondono con esso. I colori sono stati generati al computer ispirandosi alle tonalità della terra ed a quelle degli alberi locali. La spa, su due piani, offre su una superficie di 1500 metri quadrati il meritato relax dopo le escursioni in veri spettacoli naturali, come la foresta tropicale, i vulcani ed i parchi nazionali. In sale private sobriamente illuminate, vengono praticati trattamenti unici per la Costa Rica, come fanghi ricchi di minerali provenienti dalla foresta della vicina penisola di Osa.

Architect Ronald Zürcher drew inspiration from nature in his design of the resort's buildings, such as butterfly wings and armadillo shells for the property rooflines.

Der Architekt Ronald Zürcher ließ sich beim Design für seine Bauten von der Natur inspirieren, etwa von Schmetterlingsflügeln und den Panzern der Gürteltiere für die Dachsilhouetten.

Pour le design de ses édifices, l'architecte Ronald Zürcher s'est inspiré de la nature, par exemples des ailes des papillons et des carapaces des tatous pour la silhouette des toits.

A la hora de diseñar el lugar, el arquitecto Ronald Zürcher se ha dejado inspirar por la naturaleza, que se hace presente en motivos tales como alas de mariposa y caparazones de armadillo, haciendo de siluetas para el tejado.

Per il design delle sue costruzioni, l'architetto Ronald Zürcher si è lasciato ispirare dalla natura, prendendo spunto dalle ali delle farfalle o, per i contorni dei tetti, dalle corazze degli armadilli.

Built into a dramatic finger of land between two beaches, this 163-room property on the Peninsula Papagayo has wide-angle views of two Pacific Bays.

Die 163 Zimmer große Anlage wurde auf die spektakuläre Papagayo-Landzunge zwischen zwei Strände gebaut und erlaubt Panoramablicke über beide Pazifikbuchten.

Le complexe de 163 chambres a été construit entre deux plages sur la spectaculaire langue de terre de Papagayo et offre des vues panoramiques sur les deux baies du Pacifique.

Las 163 habitaciones de este enorme resort han sido construidas entre dos playas sobre la espectacular lengua de tierra de Papagayo, lanzando la vista a las dos bahías del Pacífico.

Il complesso, con 163 camere, è stato costruito sulla spettacolare lingua di terra di Papagayo, tra due spiagge, e permette un'ampia vista su entrambe le baie sul Pacifico.

Four Seasons Resort Costa Rica at Peninsula Papagayo *Peninsula Papagayo, Costa Rica*   205

El Tamarindo

Costalegre, Mexico

A rainforest resort on the Costa Alegre's southern fringe set on a 2,040-acre ecological preserve. This exclusive Mexican hideaway hotel has 28 thatched-roof bungalows that blend with the untamed beauty of the seaside tropical forest. Each serene villa has a crocheted white hammock next to its own private serpentine pool to achieve the perfect tranquil environment. The unique jungle spa offers a fine selection of special treatments under the palms or in the romantic beachfront cabaña.

Ein Resort im Regenwald am Südrand der Costa Alegre auf einem 825 Hektar großen Naturschutzgebiet. Dieses exklusive mexikanische Hideaway Hotel fügt sich mit 28 strohgedeckten Bungalows in die ungezähmte Schönheit eines Tropenwaldes am Meer ein. Die gehäkelte, weiße Hängematte neben dem privaten Serpentine-Pool sorgt in jeder der ruhigen Villen für eine angenehm entspannte Atmosphäre. Der einzigartige Dschungel-Spa unter Palmen oder in einer romantischen Cabaña am Strand hat eine Vielzahl von speziellen Behandlungen anzubieten.

Un complexe dans la forêt tropicale au Sud de la Costa Alegre sur une réserve naturelle de 825 hectares. Avec 28 bungalows recouverts de paille, ce refuge mexicain exclusif s'intègre dans la beauté d'une forêt tropicale non domptée en bord de mer. Le hamac blanc crocheté suspendu près de la piscine serpentine privée garantit une agréable atmosphère décontractée dans chaque villa au calme. L'extraordinaire Spa de la jungle sous les palmiers ou celui situé dans une cabaña romantique sur la plage propose un grand nombre de soins spéciaux.

Un resort en la selva, en el extremo sur de Costa Alegre ocupando una reserva natural de 825 hectáreas. Este exclusivo escondite mejicano funde 28 bungalows con tejado de paja en la belleza pura de la selva tropical y el mar. En las villas, las hamacas blancas trenzadas junto a una piscina en forma de serpentina transmiten una atmósfera de relajación. El inigualable Spa en la selva ofrece tratamientos especiales de los que se puede disfrutar bajo las palmeras o en una de las románticas cabañas de la playa.

Un resort nella foresta tropicale situato sul lembo meridionale della Costa Alegre su un'area protetta di 825 ettari. Questo esclusivo hotel hideaway messicano si insinua, con 28 bungalow dal tetto di paglia, nella bellezza incontaminata di una foresta tropicale sulla riva del mare. Un'amaca bianca, confezionata all'uncinetto, accanto alla sinuosa piscina, crea in ognuna delle tranquille ville una piacevole e rilassante atmosfera. La fantastica Spa, in stile giungla, sotto le palme o in una romantica cabaña sulla spiaggia, propone molti trattamenti speciali.

The lobby is as dramatic as its jungle surroundings, with a pointed thatched roof supported by peeled log poles and elliptical half-walls.

Die Lobby ist ebenso dramatisch wie der Dschungel, das spitze, strohgedeckte Dach wird von geschälten Balken und elliptischen Halbwänden getragen.

Le lobby est tout aussi dramatique que la jungle, le toit pointu et recouvert de paille est supporté par des poutres écorcées et des demi-parois elliptiques.

El vestíbulo resulta tan dramático como la selva: un tejado cubierto de paja apoyado en columnas descortezadas y medias paredes elípticas.

La lobby è coinvolgente come la giungla: il tetto a punta coperto di paglia è sostenuto da travi in legno grezzo e da mezze pareti ellittiche.

The spa's signature treatment is the cleaning ritual Temazcal, a pre-Hispanic steam bath. Guests apply an herbal healing mud wrap while resting in an igloo constructed of clay bricks

Eine Besonderheit bei den Spa-Anwendungen ist das Temazcal-Reinigungsritual — ein prä-hispanisches Dampfbad. Die Gäste ruhen in einem Iglu aus Tonziegeln, eingehüllt in eine Schlammpackung mit Kräutern.

L'une des particularités des soins Spa est le rituel de nettoyage Temazcal : un bain de vapeur pré-hispanique. Les visiteurs se reposent dans un igloo de tuiles en argiles, entourés d'une enveloppe de boue aux herbes.

El tratamiento de la casa del spa incluye el ritual de purificación Temazcal, un baño de vapor de la época prehispánica. Los huéspedes descansan cubiertos de una mezcla de barro y hierbas dentro de un iglú de ladrillos de arcilla.

Una particolarità dei trattamenti della spa è il rituale di purificazione di Temazcal — un bagno turco preispanico. Gli ospiti riposano in un igloo di tegole di terracotta, avvolti in fanghi di erbe.

Las Ventanas al Paraíso
A Rosewood Resort
Los Cabos, Mexico

Authentic hacienda-style architecture in rough stone, thatched roofs, and wrought-iron touches meets high-end indulgence. This jewel resort is a secluded desert setting with a serpentine network of infinity edge pools that disappear into the horizon. 71 spacious beachfront suites have handcrafted platform beds, terracotta fireplace and a large whirlpool with ocean views. The spa formulates a personalized experience for each guest, based on individual needs, preferences and desires.

Eine authentische Hazienda-Architektur aus rauem Stein, Strohdach und Gusseisen trifft auf Luxus der höchsten Kategorie. Dieses Resort ist eine abgeschlossene Oase in der Wüste mit einem serpentinartigen Netzwerk von Infinity-Pools, die erst hinter dem Horizont zu verschwinden scheinen. 71 weitläufige Suiten locken mit handgearbeiteten Plattformbetten, Terrakotta-Kamin und einem großen Whirlpool mit Ozeanblick. Der Spa bietet jedem Gast eine auf seine individuellen Bedürfnisse, Vorlieben und Wünsche zugeschnittene Entspannung.

L'architecture d'hacienda authentique en pierre brute, en toit de paille et en fer forgé est associée au luxe de la plus haute catégorie. Ce bijou d'hôtel est un oasis indépendant dans le désert pourvu d'un réseau de piscines panoramiques serpentines. 71 vastes suites attirent les visiteurs avec des lits plateformes faits main, une cheminée en terre cuite et un grand whirlpool avec vue sur l'océan. Le spa offre à chaque client une relaxation adaptée à ses besoins individuels, ses préférences et ses souhaits.

Una Arquitectura de hacienda auténtica consistente en piedra basta, tejado de paja y hierro forjado que encarna el lujo al más alto nivel. Esta joya de resort se ha convertido en un verdadero oasis en el desierto, con una red de piscinas serpenteantes que parecen perderse en el horizonte. Las 71 amplias suites provocan atracción gracias a sus camas de plataforma, chimenea de terracota y una grandes bañeras de hidromasaje con vistas al océano. El spa ofrece a cada huésped relax a medida, según las preferencias y necesidades personales.

L'architettura di un'autentica hacienda, di pietra grezza, con tetto di paglia e ferro battuto incontra un lusso di prima categoria. Questo gioiello di resort è un'oasi racchiusa nel deserto, con una rete di infinity pool che si snoda a zig-zag, e che sembra finire solo dietro l'orizzonte. 71 suite spaziose incantano con letti su piattaforma confezionati a mano, camino in cotto ed una grande Whirlpool con vista sull'oceano. La spa propone ad ogni ospite relax secondo le esigenze, preferenze e desideri individuali.

An open-air lounge affords vistas of stone terraces descending into the boulder-laden shoreline of miles of deserted beach.

Von der offenen Lounge eröffnen sich Blicke über die Steinterrassen, die zur der kilometerlangen, einsamen Feldsteinküste abfallen.

Le salon ouvert offre une vue imprenable sur les terrasses en bois qui mènent à la falaise déserte longue de plusieurs kilomètres.

Ante el lounge se abren amplias vistas a las terrazas de piedra que se arrojan a una kilométrica y solitaria costa de roca.

Dalla lounge aperta si apre un'ampia vista sulle terrazze in pietra, che discendono verso la lunghissima e solitaria costa pietrosa.

Las Ventanas is a flower-filled oasis of meandering waterways that spill through a series of pond.

Las Ventanas ist eine blühende Oase mäandrierender Wasserläufe, die sich in eine Abfolge von Teichen ergießen.

Las Ventanas est un oasis florissant composé de méandres de cours d'eau qui se déversent dans une succession d'étangs.

Las Ventanas es un oasis floreciente de cascadas serpenteantes que se extinguen en estanques.

Las Ventanas è un'oasi fiorita di giocose cascate che formano una serie di stagni.

212   Las Ventanas al Paraíso, A Rosewood Resort *Los Cabos, Mexico*

One&Only Palmilla

Los Cabos, Mexico

As the name suggests, this lushly landscaped property is overflowing with towering palms on a rocky promontory overlooking the Sea of Cortez. This oceanfront hacienda style resort reflects Old World architectural design with its red-tiled roofs, mosaic tile, and whitewashed stucco. Low-slung buildings are scattered throughout the exquisite gardens and vanishing ponds. The Spa is a 22,000-square-foot haven where consultants provide each guest with a personalized program in a private spa villa.

Wie der Name bereits andeutet, liegt diese Anlage unter mächtigen Palmen in großzügig gestalteter Landschaft auf einem felsigen Kap über der Cortez-See. Diese Hazienda am Meer spiegelt den Architekturstil der Alten Welt wider – Dächer mit roten Ziegeln, Mosaike und weißer Putz. Zwischen den exquisiten Gärten und verborgenen Teichen ducken sich niedrige Gebäude. Der Spa ist ein 2000 Quadratmeter großer Zufluchtsort, in dem jeder Gast mit einem persönlich zugeschnittenen Programm in privaten Spa-Villen verwöhnt wird.

Comme son nom l'indique, ce complexe a été construit sous d'imposants palmiers dans un paysage agencé à merveille sur un cap rocheux surplombant la mer Cortez. Cette hacienda en bord de mer reflète le style architectural du Vieux Monde : toits en tuiles rouges, mosaïques, et crépi blanchi. Les bâtiments peu élevés se blottissent entre les jardins exquis et les étangs camouflés. Le spa est un paradis de 2000 mètres carrés grâce auquel chaque visiteur peut bénéficier d'un programme établi sur mesure dans des villas spa privées.

Como su nombre bien indica, el resort está dominado por imponentes palmeras y un paisaje concebido a lo grande, sobre un cabo rocoso en el mar de Cortez. La hacienda a orillas del mar refleja el estilo arquitectónico del viejo mundo: tejados de teja roja, mosaicos y enlucido blanco. Entre los exquisitos jardines y estanques escondidos se dispersan edificios bajos. El spa es un refugio de 2000 metros cuadrados con villas privadas en el que se deleita a cada huésped con un programa hecho a medida.

Come dice il nome, questo complesso è situato sotto grandi palme immerse in un ricco paesaggio su un capo roccioso del mare di Cortez. Questa hacienda sul mare rispecchia lo stile architettonico del Vecchio Mondo – tetti di tegole rosse, mosaici ed intonaco bianco. I bassi edifici sono sparsi tra gli incantevoli giardini e gli stagni nascosti. La spa è un paradiso di 2000 metri quadrati, in cui ogni ospite viene viziato in ville private con un programma personalizzato.

Each of the 172 guest rooms completes the gracious style of Old Mexico with its travertine floors, handcrafted furniture, and marble bathtubs.

Jedes der 172 Gästezimmer lässt den angenehmen Stil des alten Mexikos mit Travertinfußböden, handgefertigten Möbeln und Badewannen aus Marmor aufleben.

Les 172 chambres destinées aux visiteurs font revivre le style agréable du vieux Mexique avec planchers en travertin, meubles réalisés à la main et baignoires en marbre.

Cada una de las 172 habitaciones emana el encantador estilo del viejo Méjico con sus suelos de travertino, muebles hechos a mano y bañeras de mármol.

Tutte le 172 camere lasciano rivivere il piacevole stile del vecchio Messico con pavimenti in travertino, mobili fatti a mano e vasche da bagno di marmo.

A private beach stretches below the infinity-edge pool, with lounge chairs laid out for those perfect afternoon siestas in the sun.

Unterhalb des Infinity-Pools dehnt sich der Privatstrand aus, wo Loungechairs für eine perfekte Siesta in der Sonne bereit stehen.

Sous la piscine panoramique s'étend la plage privée, où des chaises longues sont préparées pour que la sieste au soleil soit parfaite.

A los pies de la Infinity Pool se abre la playa privada en la que las tumbonas siempre están listas para una siesta al sol.

Sotto le piscine sinuose si stende la spiaggia privata, dove le loungechairs al sole invitano ad una perfetta siesta.

Index

United Kingdom

Chandler's Cross

The Grove
Chandler's Cross, Hertfordshire WD3 4TG, United Kingdom
T +44 1923 807 807, F +44 1923 221 008
www.thegrove.co.uk

227 rooms and suites. Lounge and 3 restaurants. Heated outdoor swimming pool, kid's club with children's indoor pool. Meeting facilities. 30 minutes drive from London Heathrow. Award-winning Sequoia, poolside steam room and Jacuzzi, 22 meter swimming pool.

Cowley

Cowley Manor
Cowley, Gloucestershire GL53 9NL, United Kingdom
T +44 1242 870 900, F +44 1242 870 901
www.cowleymanor.com

30 rooms. Set in 55 acres countryside. 90 minutes from London. Meeting and billiard room, film and music libraries. C-side Spa: Gym, sauna, steam room, indoor and outdoor pool all year open, hot stone treatment.

Easton Grey

Whatley Manor
Easton Grey, Malmesbury, Wiltshire SN 16 0RB, United Kingdom
T +44 1666 822 888, F +44 1666 826 120
www.whatleymanor.com

8 suites, 15 rooms, 2 restaurants. Traditional English country manor house hotel, video conference facilities. 90 minutes from London Heathrow. Spa with lounge, chamomile steam grotto, hydro therapy pool, sequenced thermal cabins and mud chamber.

Portugal

Madeira

Choupana Hills
Travessa do Largo da Choupana, 9060-348 Funchal, Madeira, Portugal
T +351 291 206 020, F +351 291 206 021
www.choupanahills.com

64 rooms including 4 suites. Xôpana Restaurant, Basalt Bar and lounge. On the hills overlooking the city of Funchal and the ocean. 20 minutes from the airport. Health and beauty Spa: Interior and exterior pool, aromatherapy and hydro massage. Rasul, hamam and sauna. Gym, yoga, body treatments and facials.

Switzerland

Geneva

La Réserve Genève Hotel and Spa
301, route de Lausanne, 1293 Genève, Switzerland
T +41 22 959 5959, F +41 22 959 5960
www.lareserve.ch

102 rooms and suites. Located on the right shore of Lake Geneva. 5 km from the center of Geneva and 3 km from the International Airport. Spa: 17 treatment rooms, art gym, indoor and outdoor pool, sauna, hamam. Facial and beauty treatments, La Prairie and Cinq Mondes.

Interlaken

Victoria-Jungfrau Grand Hotel & Spa
Höheweg 41, 3800 Interlaken, Switzerland
T +41 33 828 2828, F +41 33 828 2880
www.victoria-jungfrau.ch

222 rooms and suites, restaurants and bars, Tower Suite, conferences and banquets. Situated in Bernese Oberland. 45 minutes from Bern airport and 2 hours from Zurich. ESPA treatments, Clarins Beauty Center, day spa, Taiji and Quigong.

Italy

Milan

Bulgari Hotels & Resorts Milano
Via Privata Fratelli Gabba 7/b, 20121 Milan, Italy
T +39 02 805 805 1, F +39 02 805 805 222
www.bulgarihotels.com

58 rooms and suites, the majority of them overlook the 4000 square meter private garden. Gold mosaic swimming pool. ESPA: massages, shiatsu, stone therapy, steam room, pre/post natal treatment, jet-lag eliminator massages.

Greece

Thessaloniki

Kempinski Hotel Nikopolis
16–18, Asklipiou Str. – Pylea, P.O. Box 60019, 57001 Thermi, Thessaloniki, Greece
T +30 2310 401 000, F +30 2310 401 094
www.kempinski-thessaloniki.com

99 rooms including 7 suites, 1 Presidential Suite, restaurant, bar, 20,000 square meter garden. Located in the business district. 10 km from the fair center. 3 km from Macedonia International Airport. Kempinski Spa: sauna, steam rooms, Jacuzzi, private treatment rooms.

Turkey

Bodrum

Kempinski Hotel Barbaros Bay
Kizilagac Koyu, Gerenkuyu Mevkii Yaliciftlik, 48400 Bodrum, Turkey
T +90 252 3110303, F +90 252 3110303
www.kempinski-bodrum.com

148 rooms, 25 suites, 8 restaurants and bars. Views over the bay and Aegean Sea, 30 minutes from Bodrum International Airport. Six Senses Spa with principles of Feng Shui. 5500 square meter private spa area which can be rented. Watsu based treatment.

Morocco

Marrakech

Amanjena
Route de Quarzazate, Km 12, 40000 Marrakech, Morocco
T +212 4 440 3353, F +212 4 440 3477
www.amanjena.com

32 pavilions with fireplace, private pool and garden. 6 Maisons. Al-Hamra Suite, 180 square meter pavilion, 2 minzahs and its own 40 square meter pool. 5 miles south of the center of Marrakech. Spa: Heated swimming pool. With 2 hamams, steam bath, massages, manicures, pedicures and facials.

United Arab Emirates

Dubai

Al Maha Desert Resort & Spa
Sheikh Zayed Road, Dubai, United Arab Emirates
T +971 4 303 4222, F +971 4 343 9696
www.al-maha.com

Built in the style of a traditional Bedouin encampment. 37 Bedouin Suites, 2 Royal Suites and 1 Emirates Suite. Conference facilities for up to 90 persons. 45 minutes from Dubai International Airport. Jamilah Spa: Hydrotherapy and rasul rooms, sauna, Jacuzzi, ice-cold plunge pool.

Dubai

Madinat Jumeirah
P.O. Box 75157, Dubai, United Arab Emirates
T +971 4 366 8888, F +971 4 366 7788
www.madinatjumeirah.com

Resort: Arabian village style, comprises 867 rooms and suites including 2 boutique hotels and 29 Traditional Courtyard Summer Houses. 44 restaurants. 25 minutes from Dubai International Airport. Six Senses Spa: 26 designed treatment rooms. Outdoor treatment tents, sauna, steam rooms, Jacuzzi and plunge pool.

Dubai

One&Only Royal Mirage
P.O. Box 37252, Dubai, United Arab Emirates
T +971 4 399 9999, F +971 4 399 9998
www.oneandonlyresorts.com

The resort comprises 3 properties: The Palace (226 rooms and 20 suites with balcony or terrace), Arabian Court (162 rooms and 10 suites with balcony or terrace), Residence & Spa (3 royal villas, 18 suites and 32 deluxe rooms). 20 minutes from Dubai International Airport. Health club, Givenchy Spa, hamam.

Mauritius

Trou d'Eau Douce

One&Only Le Touessrok
Trou d'Eau Douce, Mauritius
T +230 402 7400, F +230 402 7500
www.oneandonlyresorts.com

68 Deluxe rooms, 132 suites, restaurants and bars. The Resort is on the east coast of the island, 50 minutes from the airport and the capital Port Louis. Givenchy Spa works with fitness center trainers and with Bastien Gonzalez Podiatry & Pedicure Clinic.

South Africa

Hermanus

The Western Cape Hotel & Spa
Arabella Country Estate, R44, Kleinmond, Overberg, Western Cape, South Africa
T +27 28 284 0000, F +27 28 284 0011
www.arabellasheraton.co.za

145 rooms and suites including 2 presidential suites. 2 restaurants. 60 minutes drive from Cape Town International Airport. AltiraSPA: Hamam; brine, plunge and lap pool. Jacuzzi, Rasul chamber, steam room, sauna, hydro pool complex, fitness center and yoga.

India

Jaipur

Oberoi Rajvilas

Goner Road, Jaipur, Rajasthan 303 012, India
T +91 141 268 0101, F +91 141 268 0202
www.oberoihotels.com

54 rooms, 14 luxury tents, two one-bedroom pool villas, one two-bedroom Royal Villa. Conference facilities. 40 minutes from Jaipur airport. Oberoi Spa by Banyan Tree offers personalized ayurvedic treatments, steam room, sauna, Jacuzzi, heated outside pool and yoga.

Udaipur

Oberoi Udaivilas

Haridasji Ki Magri, Udaipur, Rajasthan 313 001, India
T +91 294 243 3300, F +91 294 243 3200
www.oberoihotels.com

86 rooms and suites including 3 suites with pool. Kohinoor Suite with pool, open fireplace and sauna. 45 minutes from Udaipur airport. Oberoi Spa by Banyan Tree with Ayurvedic, Thai and Western techniques. 5 double spa suites, steam room, sauna and beauty salon.

Uttaranchal

Ananda in the Himalayas

The Palace Estate, Narendra Nagar, Tehri-Garhwal, Uttaranchal 249 175, India
T +91 1378 227 500, F +91 1378 227 550
www.anandaspa.com

70 deluxe rooms and 5 suites. restaurants, 1 spa restaurant, tea lounge. 260 km north of New Delhi, 45 minutes flight to Jolly Grant airport. Spa: Massages, water therapy, Ayurveda, exfoliation, body wraps, skin care, yoga.

Maldives

South Malé Atoll

Cocoa Island

Makunufushi, South Malé Atoll, Maledives
T +960 441 818, F +960 441 919
www.cocoa-island.com

17 suites and 16 villas with private sun decks. Sunset villa with private jetty. Fully equipped dive center, water sports. 30 minutes by speedboat from Malé International Airport. COMO Shambhala retreat: massages, scrubs, marine algae wraps and bath. Daily program of yoga, meditation and movement exercises.

North Malé Atoll

One&Only Maldives at Reethi Rah

Reethi Rah, North Malé Atoll, Maldives
T +960 664 88 00, F +960 664 88 22
www.oneandonlyresorts.com

130 villas, each occupying its own secluded piece of sandy shore or private deck. Restaurants and in-villa dining. View over the ocean. 35 km from Malé International Airport. ESPA: Steam rooms, stone saunas, hot pools with shoulder massages and Chi Pavilion for yoga and pilates.

Bhutan

Paro

Uma Paro

P.O. Box 222, Paro, Buthan
T +975 8 271 597, F +975 8 271 513
www.uma.como.bz

20 rooms and nine villas. All rooms have views of the forest, mountain or valley. Located on a 38-acre site atop a tree-clad hill. Close to the town of Paro where the nation's only airport is. COMO Shambhala: Acupuncture, reflexology, traditional bath, Ayurveda, massage therapy and yoga.

Hong Kong

Hong Kong

The Plateau

Grand Hyatt Hong Kong
1 Harbour Road, Hong Kong
T +852 2584 7688, F +852 2584 7738
www.plateau.com.hk

Plateau is the Spa of the Grand Hyatt. It accommodates 23 guest rooms and suites, 2 restaurants, 1 private function room. Spa & fitness, also day spa. Deluxe treatment rooms. Products: Carita, Decleor, Shiffa, June Jacobs and Aesop. Treatments: Shiatsu, Chinese, Swedish, Thai, reflexology.

Hong Kong

The Landmark

Mandarin Oriental Hong Kong
15 Queens Road Central, Hong Kong
T +852 2132 0188, F +852 2132 0199
www.mandarinoriental.com/landmark

113 rooms and suites, Amber, MO Bar and Spa Café. 40 minutes by car to Hong Kong International Airport. The Oriental Spa: 15 private deluxe treatment rooms, VIP spa suites. Rainforest showers, vitality pool, amethyst crystal steam room, Rasul, laconium, hamam, sauna and Zen relaxation room.

Taiwan

Sun Moon Lake

The Lalu

142 Jungshing Road, Yuchr Siang Nantou, 555 R.O.C., Taiwan
T +888 49 285 5311, F +888 49 285 5312
www.thelalu.com.tw

96 rooms, suites and villas including a presidential suite. 3 restaurants, lounge and Chinese teahouse. The Lalu Spa: Massages, steam and sauna facilities. overlooking Sun Moon Lake.

South Korea

Seoul

Park Hyatt Seoul

995-14 Daechi 3-dong, Gangnam-gu, Seoul 135-502, South Korea
T +82 2 2016 1234, F +82 2 2016 1200
www.seoul.park.hyatt.com

185 rooms with spa-inspired bathrooms including a 15-inch flat-screen tv. Situated opposite the Seoul Convention and Exhibition Centre (COEX). Spa, fitness center (23rd floor) and indoor heated swimming pool (24th floor) with views across Seoul.

Thailand

Bangkok

Grand Hyatt Erawan Bangkok

494 Rajdamri Road, Bangkok 10330, Thailand
T +66 2 254 1234, F +66 2 254 6308
www.bangkok.grand.hyatt.com

380 rooms. 9 restaurants. Located in the city center, 30 minutes from Bangkok International Airport. i.sawan Residential Spa & Club: 6 Spa cottages, 9 treatment bungalows, Jacuzzi, steam room, cold plunge, sauna and 25 meter swimming pool.

Chiang Mai

Mandarin Oriental Dhara Dhevi

51/4 Chiang Mai, Sankampaeng Road Moo 1 T. Tasala A. Muang, Chiang Mai 50000, Thailand
T +66 53 888 929, F +66 53 888 928
www.mandarinoriental.com/chiangmai

123 suites, pavilions and villas. Open terraces, some of which feature private pool. 15 minutes to Chiang Mai International Airport. 3000 square meter Dheva Spa, 25 treatment rooms and suites, spa menu, treatments that are inherent to the Lanna culture.

Hua Hin

Evason Hideaway & Six Senses Spa at Hua Hin

9/22 Moo 5, Paknampran Beach, Prachuap Khiri Khan 77220, Thailand
T +66 32 618 200, F +66 32 618 201
www.sixsenses.com/hideaway-huahin

Each of the 55 villas has its own private pool, outdoor bath and beautifully landscaped garden. 3 hours from Bangkok or 35 minutes by air shuttle. The Earth Spa by Six Senses comprises a cluster of 9 buildings, which appear to be floating on ponds.

Koh Samui

Sila Evason Hideaway & Spa at Samui

9/10 Moo 5, Baan Plai Lam, Bophut, Koh Samui Suratthani 84320, Thailand
T +66 77 245 678, F +66 77 245 671
www.sixsenses.com/hideaway-samui

66 villas, most with private infinity-edge pool. 10 minutes from Koh Samui Airport and 20 minutes to 18-hole golf course. Spa with outdoor and indoor treatment, beauty salon, 2 dry saunas, 2 steam rooms, gym.

Koh Samui

Sala Samui Resort and Spa

10/9 Moo 5, Baan Plai Lam, Bophut, Koh Samui Suratthani 84320, Thailand
T +66 77 245 888, F +66 77 245 889
www.salasamui.com

69 rooms total with 53 private swimming pools, 2 beachfront swimming pools. Library, Internet & center, boardroom. 10 minutes from Koh Samui Airport. Mandara Spa: 2 double spa suites and 2 double deluxe rooms. Traditional Thai massages, body scrubs, indoor or outside treatment.

Vietnam

Nha Trang

Evason Hideaway & Six Senses Spa at Ana Mandara

c/o Beachside Tran Phu Blvd, Nha Trang, Vietnam
T +84 58 524 705, F +84 58 524 704
www.sixsenses.com/hideaway-anamandara

35 beach villas, 5 hill top villas, 5 water villas with rockery, 4 rock villas, 5 spa suite villas, 1 presidential villa. Restaurant, bar. 25 minutes from Nha Trang Airport. Six Senses Spa: 6 treatment rooms, yoga pavilion, steam and sauna facilities, spa herbal garden, tennis, water sports, diving facilities and gym.

Singapore

Indonesia

Australia

California

Florida

West Indies

Costa Rica

Mexico

Photo Credits

Editors   Patrice Farameh
Martin Nicholas Kunz

Editorial Coordination   Patricia Massó

Hotel Texts by   Patrice Farameh, Rosina Geiger,
Bärbel Holzberg

Imaging   Tobias Schimpf, Jeremy Ellington

Translations by   SAW Communications,
Dr. Sabine A. Werner (Hotel Texts)
and Ade-Team Stuttgart
(Cover Text and Introduction)
English   Dr. Suzanne Kirkbright (SAW)
German   Dr. Wolfgang Hensel (SAW),
Claudia Ade (Ade-Team)
French   Céline Verschelde (SAW),
Jocelyne Abarca (Ade-Team)
Spanish   Carmen de Miguel (SAW),
Sara Costa-Sengera (Ade-Team)
Italian   Maria-Letizia Haas (SAW),
Jacqueline Rizzo (Ade-Team)

Editorial project by fusion publishing gmbh, stuttgart . los angeles
www.fusion-publishing.com

Published by teNeues Publishing Group

teNeues Verlag GmbH + Co. KG
Am Selder 37, 47906 Kempen, Germany
Tel.: 0049-(0)2152-916-0, Fax: 0049-(0)2152-916-111
Press department: arehn@teneues.de

teNeues Publishing Company
16 West 22nd Street, New York, NY 10010, USA
Tel.: 001-212-627-9090, Fax: 001-212-627-9511

teNeues Publishing UK Ltd.
P.O. Box 402, West Byfleet, KT14 7ZF, Great Britain
Tel.: 0044-1932-403509, Fax: 0044-1932-403514

teNeues France S.A.R.L.
93, rue Bannier, 45000 Orléans, France
Tel.: 0033-2-38541071, Fax: 0033-2-38625340

www.teneues.com

© 2007 teNeues Verlag GmbH + Co. KG, Kempen

Second Edition

ISBN: 978-3-8327-9108-7

Printed in Italy

Bibliographic information published by Die Deutsche Bibliothek.
Die Deutsche Bibliothek lists this publication in the Deutsche
Nationalbibliografie; detailed bibliographic data is available in the
Internet at http://dnb.ddb.de